ART OF THE CLIMB

EVERY PROFESSIONAL'S GUIDEBOOK FOR EXCELLING AND WINNING IN A CORPORATE CAREER

C. Venugopal

Chennai • Bangalore

CLEVER FOX PUBLISHING
Chennai, India

Published by CLEVER FOX PUBLISHING 2023
Copyright © C.Venugopal 2023

All Rights Reserved.
ISBN: 978-93-56485-03-7

This book has been published with all reasonable efforts taken to make the material error-free after the consent of the author. No part of this book shall be used, reproduced in any manner whatsoever without written permission from the author, except in the case of brief quotations embodied in critical articles and reviews.

The Author of this book is solely responsible and liable for its content including but not limited to the views, representations, descriptions, statements, information, opinions and references ["Content"]. The Content of this book shall not constitute or be construed or deemed to reflect the opinion or expression of the Publisher or Editor. Neither the Publisher nor Editor endorse or approve the Content of this book or guarantee the reliability, accuracy or completeness of the Content published herein and do not make any representations or warranties of any kind, express or implied, including but not limited to the implied warranties of merchantability, fitness for a particular purpose. The Publisher and Editor shall not be liable whatsoever for any errors, omissions, whether such errors or omissions result from negligence, accident, or any other cause or claims for loss or damages of any kind, including without limitation, indirect or consequential loss or damage arising out of use, inability to use, or about the reliability, accuracy or sufficiency of the information contained in this book.

CONTENTS

Introduction iv

Starting the Climb **1**
   1. The First Steps 2
   2. Is There a Job Looking for You? 13
   3. When Do You Leave a Job? 32
   4. The Rungs of the Ladder 44

Hazards of the Climb **54**
   5. Does Your Boss Like You? 55
   6. The Indian Rope Trick 67
   7. Results Matter 80
   8. Behavior Matters Even More 90

The Final Ascent **102**
   9. Stress: The Career Killer 103
  10. Everest Base Camp 115
  11. Race to the Top 125
  12. New Beginnings 137

Summary of Chapters 145
About the Author 158

INTRODUCTION

"*W*ho are you?" This is an existential question. But ask this question to most people and the reply you get would be: *I am a software engineer* or *I am General Manager Marketing, XYZ Inc* or *I am a content writer* or *I am a corporate trainer*. You see an old man walking in the park and if you pop the same question, *Who are you?* You will most probably get the reply, *I am a retired bank officer*, or an answer in a similar vein, referring to a past profession.

As human beings, we seem to define ourselves wholly based on our careers. Is this right? Are we not multifaceted individuals? Is a career the only or best way to define who we are? Probably not; but, for most people, a career is a very important part of who they think they are. And till we reach a stage of maturity to define ourselves more meaningfully, a career becomes our principal identity.

Why this is so, is self-evident. We spend the first twenty-odd years of our lives preparing for our careers. The next 30 to 40 years are spent in the career and the decades that follow are lived out of the earnings of the career. Even our friendships, sometimes our spouses, and of course our reputations are acquired and nurtured during our careers. Careers, indeed, make us what we are.

Careers sometimes break people too. There are many who are miserable in a career and are just waiting for the opportunity to chuck it all away and retire into a "happier" life. Careers can stress people to the point of heart attacks. Often, instead of friendships, bitter enmities follow careers. While careers challenge people to produce their best, they also test the moral and ethical fibre of people like none other. The best fall prey to ambition. The opposing demands of corporate profits on the one hand and ethical practices on the other, test the character of many heads of businesses.

Careers need to be managed. But, many realize this truth only after a few hard knocks or when it is too late to correct. *If only I had a career coach in my thirties,* laments a forty-year-old as he faces yet another year of no promotions. *I wish someone had told me how to handle difficult bosses,* says the young executive, who had just left his or her third company bitterly. This book is designed to be *that coach.*

I have had a long corporate career of nearly three decades. This was followed by another decade and a half as an advisor, coach and consultant to scores of companies and professionals including leadership teams. During my career, I had good bosses and bad bosses, happy days and depressing days, challenging moments and those of dullness and boredom. My career had its ups and downs.

It is these experiences that made my consulting and coaching career so eventful and rewarding. I could look back at my good and bad career moments with perspective and learn from them. In the troubles faced by my coaching and consulting clients, I could see shades of the same dilemma and anguish I had faced. I could gently lead my clients to introspect and reframe their career canvases to greater effectiveness. When they got their *ah-ha* moments and were able to break free from their shackles and bloom in their careers, I was the happiest. Having a great and rewarding career is everyone's right. My job was to help them see the way.

This book is a result of my long years of experience as a career professional and consultant. It is limited to corporate careers and does not include in its ambit individual careers as that of a musician or lawyer or artist. It also does not include an entrepreneurial career. That is covered in my earlier book, *BYOB: Be Your Own Boss*. This book is restricted to those who have to navigate the labyrinth of a corporate career.

This book uses two metaphors to understand a corporate career. The first likens the career to a mountain climb which needs skill and tact to deal with the hazards on the way. The second metaphor is that of a game of Snakes and Ladders. Just as in the game, in a career one encounters opportunities that take you forward and unseen snakes that drive you to the bottom. These metaphors are interspersed throughout the book.

Different stages of a career require different skill sets to excel. This book, therefore, is divided into three sections, with four chapters in each. The first section, *Starting the Climb*, is about the first few years of a career. It deals with the issue of getting the first job and starting the journey. It also discusses when to leave a job and explains the structure of the corporate hierarchy. The next section, *Hazards of the Climb*, deals with issues like bad bosses, damaging behavior and such obstacles that need to be tackled. The last section, *The Final Ascent*, explains the last stages of the career journey and the years beyond.

Like life, a career is a long journey. All start together, but some manage to go farther. Goals may differ, change, and sometimes stay distant and unattained at the end. But that doesn't matter. What matters is the journey. Some enjoy it and some don't. We believe that all should enjoy the career journey. This book is designed to help the professional not just win the career game but also enjoy it while it lasts.

STARTING THE CLIMB

1

THE FIRST STEPS

*E*veryone starts the climb of the corporate ladder with the first step but true success comes to those who master the *Art of the Climb*. It is not the brightest or the best who rise to the top in organizations; it is those who wisely negotiate the twists and turns on the way.

A corporate career is a labyrinth, full of surprises—headwinds that stall and tailwinds that open opportunities. The path ahead is unclear—some leading to dead ends and others to grand vistas. And to top it all, the goalpost keeps shifting throughout the journey. Mastering the *Art of the Climb* is the only way to stay ahead. Let us understand this with a story:

Kunal topped his classes at IIT and IIM, an allrounder—good in sports, a great orator, and a born leader. He was selected as a management trainee (MT) in a leading MNC and dived into his career with gusto. Kunal came out at the top in his batch of MTs at the end of the training.

The company spotted him as a star who could grow to general management and C-level roles. He was given prime assignments to hone his leadership skills to prepare for senior management. Everyone expected great things from young Kunal.

Kunal did do well, but he fell just short of making it to his potential. After good growth in the first five years, far ahead of others in his batch, his growth trajectory plateaued. After another five years of average growth, he was side-lined to a staff role. Fifteen years into his career, he was languishing.

In contrast, his friend Aravind, who was far less "worthy" (he had only made it as a waitlisted candidate) had an average first five years but soon his career accelerated. In 15 years, while Kunal was stuck in a senior management role, Aravind was promoted to the board by the age of 38. Kunal, the potential star, left the company in his forties.

What had happened to Kunal? Why did he falter in the climb? He had started well, but something happened along the way. It could be one of several things. He probably had a habit or behavior that irritated people. Maybe, it was a boss who put in that negative remark in his appraisal. Perhaps, it was an assignment that didn't go well. The fact is Kunal didn't manage the climb well and despite his innate potential, did not reach the heights he could have.

Looking back at his career, Kunal often wishes that he had an advisor or coach who could have steered him in the right direction.

If only I had not made those avoidable mistakes, Kunal always laments. Most often these "mistakes" are not related to technical skills or results, they are related to:

- Rubbing a boss or some other influential person the wrong way

- Creating enemies among colleagues
- Misreading a situation and landing into an avoidable mess
- Lack of control of the tongue (or fingers in the case of e-mails fights)
- Insensitive behavior
- Shifting priorities

All these can be addressed if detected and understood on time. The purpose of this book is to make you, the career aspirant, aware of these hazards on the climb and to suggest ways to avoid them.

This book is your coach to help you manage the climb.

What is a career?

A career is not a series of 100-meter sprints, it is more akin to a marathon or an Ironman race that needs strategy, stamina, endurance, and most of all, maturity. You may meet unexpected hazards on the way. There could be tempting side roads that could lead you astray. Though all start together, many would get ahead of you and many behind. Handling the pressure of overtaking the runners in front and at the same time, treating those behind with respect is a key determinant for success. In your career, as in the race, your ability to recognize and deal with hazards, the maturity to avoid dangerous shortcuts, the grit to bear the pain at times, and above all your maturity, determines if you emerge a winner or a loser.

While a career is like a marathon in many ways, there is a significant difference. In the race, the goal is the same for all, but a career could have different endpoints. Moreover, this goal would change as the career progresses. Everybody cannot become CEO; there is place for only one at the top. Everybody cannot rise to senior management; there are limited spots available. So, even if people start at the same point, the endpoint would be different for each person. Like in an army, all start as officer cadets, but some rise to be majors, some to colonels, some get command and the chosen few get to wear the four stars.

Therefore, while you fix your goal in the beginning, re-evaluating, and changing the goal, as you progress, is equally important in managing a career successfully. The goal for all is the pursuit of happiness. A career is a means to achieving this goal. The journey is the pursuit and it should also be happy. Irrespective of where one reaches finally, if the journey has, by and large, been happy, then you have succeeded. Everybody can and should aim for a happy and contended journey as it is the journey that consumes most of your life.

Having said this, let us understand the complex issue of career goals.

Career Goals

Why do we have a career? Of course, to earn a living. But that is not all. It is far more complex. In a lifetime, twenty years or more are spent preparing for a career, forty years or more in it, and the final years living off the earnings from the career. Equally, if not more important, are the friendships, reputation, and position earned during the career.

What does it profit a man to end a career with a big bank balance, if on the way he/she leaves behind fractured relationships, enemies, and a poor reputation?

What do you want from a career? We asked this simple question to a wide variety of respondents. Their answers were different and sometimes intriguing.

Here is a sample of the responses.

What do you want from a career? *(responses from a survey done)*

- To earn a good livelihood
- To pass time *(this was a response from the daughter of a well-to-do businessman)*
- To have a good family life
- To get a good wife[1] *(village kids had the option to continue working in the fields or work in a factory away from home. Working in a reputed firm apparently raised their status in the marriage market!)*
- To get away from an oppressive home environment *(many housewives see a career as a stress buster. For those ten hours, away from home, they are in a place where they are respected, meet new people, and have a voice of their own).*
- To reach a position and gain respect in society
- To make an impact on the world
- To earn enough to enjoy life after retirement
- To gain expertise and expand knowledge
- To earn a lot of money to get the freedom to do whatever I want
- To sharpen my knowledge and grow as a person

As you can see, everyone approaches a career with different goals. If you ask 50 persons, you may get 50 different career goals. But,

---

[1] This is not just restricted to men. Even women find that their marriage prospects increase if they are in a career. Therefore, probably this response should be generalized to " to get a good partner!"

these diverse goal statements can be clustered around five broad goals. These are:

1. Security and livelihood
2. Comfort and well-being for self and family
3. Improved social standing and respect
4. Professional and personal development
5. Self-Actualization: to realize one's fullest potential as a human being

Though these are the common goals for a career, the importance attached to each would defer from person to person. One person may see a career only as a means to a good living, nothing more. Another person may want respect and influence more than anything else from a career. Yet, another may want to leave a mark in his or her professional circle.

What we seek from a career may change as we grow older in it. When a person joins, he or she may want to rise to be the CEO. With time, they realize that the effort needed to reach the very top is too much and they would much rather leave the stress and hard work to someone else. They may be content to stay at lower levels which provides them more time with their families or allows them to pursue a hobby or an alternate calling.

A career goal is a personal choice. Like most other goals in life, career goals also call for trade-offs. You may prefer to stay in a city you are comfortable with, rather than take that project opportunity that requires a shift. You may choose to rise in a career through the technical expertise or specialist route, rather than take on managerial roles that may bring in a different set of challenges. You may even decide to step off the roller coaster career ride, for a sabbatical or a stint with an NGO. All of these are your choices to make. This book helps you get clarity on your goals and pursue your career within those boundaries.

The first step is to evaluate your career journey, at this point of time. This would help you take stock and make course corrections if needed. A book of this kind is not just a nice-to-know book. It is a book that would change the trajectory of your career. For this purpose, in most chapters, there are exercises and there are questions for you to ponder over. Doing these exercises and thinking of the questions posed would make the reading of this book more purposeful and effective.

Let us start with an exercise to help you understand your career aspirations, at this point. Remember that nothing is written in stone. Your aspirations may change, and there is nothing wrong with that. If you know what they are, there is a greater chance that you will achieve them.

Exercise 1.1 Career Goals Assessment

Career Goals					
	Importance Levels				
GOALS	**High -5**	**4**	**3**	**2**	**Low -1**
Earnings					
Family comfort and well being					
Social Standing					
Professional Development					
Self-Actualization					

Look back at your career, as of now and introspect. Mark the level of importance you attach for each of the goals in the template above. You are trying to find the relative priority of each of the goals, for you. Please remember that there is always a trade-off. One goal could come at the cost of the other. Therefore, try to be honest and mark the above table to reflect your true needs for a career.

There is no right or wrong in this. For each person, a career means different things. This exercise helps you assess your career aspirations at this point of time. As said earlier, this could change with time and there is nothing wrong with that either. Just be honest—it works best that way.

Resist the temptation to mark each as equally important, at around the middle of the scale as this does not help. You are trying to capture the *relative importance* of each of these goals in your life. One way to do this is to assign numbers 5 to 1, from the most to the least important among all the above. This forces you to prioritize among the list of goals. That is, assign 5 to what you consider as the most important, 4 to what you consider as the next most important, and so on. This will give you a good idea of the priorities in your mind.

After you have done this reflect once again on your choices. Do you want to make any changes?

Is your ladder of success placed right?

Now that you have assessed your career goals, you need to check if your current path is taking you there. Often, we have a goal, but our current path or actions are taking us away from the goal. The following quote from Thomas Merton, an American sociologist, thinker, and writer puts this very well.

> *People may spend their whole life climbing the ladder of success, only to find, once they reach the top, that the ladder was leaning against the wrong wall.*
>
> **– Thomas Merton**

Relook at your career status now. Consider your position, the type of work, the kind of company and colleagues, and your level of earnings. Are you doing the things that would take you closer to the goal or away from it? Is your ladder leaning against the right wall?

How do you know if your ladder is leaning against the right wall? The questions in Exercise 1.2 would help you determine this.

Exercise 1.2: Long-Term Goal Alignment

1. Am I in the right direction to meet my career goals?
2. Will the activities that I am doing now give me the right learning and experience to take me to my goal?
3. Is my current job aligned with my goal? If yes, great. If not, is it at least taking me closer to the goal?
4. Is my current job/career taking me away from my goal? (*For example, if your key goal was to be close to family and their comfort and you are in a job that requires 20 days of travel, surely you are going away from your goal, right?*)
5. Am I happy with my career choice/position? (*Remember that even if not stated explicitly, the pursuit of happiness is everybody's goal.*)

These questions seen along with your career goals (Exercise 1.1) will tell you whether there is alignment between what you want from your career and where you are now. If you have answered "yes" to all the questions (except Q 4) , then you are goal-aligned. If not, you need to take a new look at where your career is taking you.

If you see alignment, then you know that you should continue along the same path. But if you find that all your actions are taking you away from your stated goal, then you know there is a problem. This dissonance will cause stress in your life. There would be a continuous struggle in your mind that would prevent you from enjoying your job and even performing it as well as you should. If this is the case, you know it is time to act. Goal alignment is key to mastering the *Art of the Climb*.

The Right Goals: Aspirational but Realistic

Sometimes, we set lofty goals for ourselves. They may indeed be aspirational, but are they realistic? Let me share a bit of my story:

I joined a new firm in my early thirties in a mid-management position. We had a system of annual appraisals. It had a self-appraisal section with the standard question, "Where do you see yourself five years from now?"

I answered with all sincerity, "I see myself as the executive director (ED)." The executive director was a very senior position in the company. The incumbent at that time was five levels above me and twenty years older. It was impossible to reach that level in five years (in those days, promotions were slow and far between).

But I was brazenly confident of my potential and had no hesitation to put this down in my appraisal. Of course, I didn't make it to that level in five years, not even in the next ten years. Yet, in every appraisal in those five years and beyond, I would write the same answer to the question.

Looking back, I realize how foolish I was. I am sure the head of HR would have laughed at my naivety. This overestimation of self may have made me look pompous and prevented me from even achieving the levels I could have. Also, looking back, I realize that I didn't put in the effort needed for accelerated growth. I was just a dreamer without the grit to make my dreams come true.

Your goals must be aspirational to motivate. But, at the same time, they must be realistic. You must also be prepared to put in the hard work needed to achieve the goal. The first step in managing the climb is to have aspirational but realistic goals *followed up with the right action and efforts* to achieve the same.

A career is made up of a series of steps: jobs, assignments, and responsibilities. These may be in one firm or multiple firms. You may start in one, move through the levels, and rise to the top or you may hop jobs, each taking you higher and higher up the ladder. Whichever route you take, it is important that each career change (*in the same company or a new one*) is a strategic move in your climb. Great careers are built step by step, strategically.

But how do you get the right jobs or job roles to build such a career? Read on…

2

IS THERE A JOB LOOKING FOR YOU?

*W*hy is a job search so tedious? You ask any recruiter, at any firm, and you will hear the lament about how difficult it is to get the right candidate, at any level. Talk to job aspirants, and you will hear the same lament, in reverse-*where have all the good jobs gone?* The same is the case, *within a firm*. Managers are fighting for talent and the talent is yearning for that great assignment. Projects demand people, while talent languishes on the bench.

This is the challenge and the dilemma. Candidates and jobs are in search of (but not finding), each other. Recruitment firms enjoy and make their living out of this. Everyone is always searching.

But why this frenzy?

The search process takes long and is tedious because both the job seeker and the employer, *approach the search differently*. This is best explained in a classic book, *What Color is Your Parachute?* by

Richard N Bolles, written in 1970 with over 55 revisions since that date. This book is one of the all-time 100 best non-fiction books and has sold millions of copies. All job seekers, irrespective of level, would find value in this book.

Some of the key ideas of the book are summarized below:

- Job seekers and employers think differently. If you need to be successful in the game, you must understand this difference and act accordingly.
- Job seekers almost always follow the same route for a job hunt: resumes, using search agencies/job portals, and responding to job advertisements. Employers, on the other hand, keep changing strategies depending on the job market.
- If the job market is good for candidates (*more jobs than candidates*), the employer uses the typical route of resumes and search consultants. When the job market is tight (*more candidates than jobs*), the employer stops reading the resumes and posting vacancies. They follow different tactics to recruit. *They play the elimination game.*
- The candidate wants to get hired and so, he/she spruces up the resume and keeps sending them out. The employer wants to *eliminate*—reduce the pile of 1000+ resumes to the two or three they want to interview. Your resume, therefore, would most likely get eliminated very early in the game, *even though you may be as eligible as those shortlisted.*
- One of the most interesting ideas in the book is the employer's order of preference for the vacancy-filling process. The employer's 1st preference is to promote from within; *searching through resumes is the last choice.* On the

other hand, for a candidate, sending out a resume is the first choice because it is the easiest (see Table 2.1).

Table 2.1: Vacancy Filling Differences

Differences in the vacancy filling process		
Vacancy filling method	Job seeker's Preference	Employers Preference
Using the resume	1	6
Job Ad	2	5
Search Agency	3	4
Referrals	4	3
Experience proof	5	2
From within	6	1

To be successful the job seeker must also change tactics depending on the kind of job market. He/she must ensure that they are on the shortlist when the employer is on an elimination spree. This is done by ensuring, (1) the right keywords are used in the resume, (2) the resume is drafted with care and is concise and precise, and (3) the cover letter is drafted keeping in mind the perceived needs of the job and the employer.

Candidates rely on resumes/portals and search agencies; employers prefer to fill vacancies either internally or through the referral of a trusted employee or colleague.

Do you see the mismatch? You send out resumes, but the employer prefers to promote an internal candidate or recruit through referrals. Therefore, if you want that job, you need to change your tactics. Here are a few takeaways to be kept in mind.

Key Takeaways

1. Employers prefer to fill up vacancies internally[2]. Therefore, you should aim to get that internal promotion in your current company. It may be easier than looking for the rise outside your company. Be on the lookout for opportunities within your company. Develop good contacts in the HR department to alert you on such vacancies. Be on the good books of seniors across departments. Create a persona for yourself as a useful, resourceful and efficient person.
2. Getting somebody to refer you, is better than sending out a resume or using a search agency. Use social media platforms like LinkedIn to connect to persons in your target company *(valuable tip:* reach out to people you may only vaguely know or even not know. You would be surprised at the number of persons who would be willing to help).
3. If you are responding to a job ad by using a resume, ensure that it doesn't get eliminated by (i) making it short and sharp (ii) using correct keywords that appear in the job description (JD), and (iii) highlighting job-specific experience.

Job Search Preparations

The standard steps to get your dream job are (1) writing the perfect resume, (2) cracking the interview, and (3) negotiating for salary and position. Let us look at these steps in some detail:

---

[2] Research shows that it costs 30% or more of the candidate's yearly CTC, to get a new candidate for a job. So, companies often prefer to promote internally than recruit.

Writing the Perfect Resume

A resume is the first document that introduces you to your potential employer. It must make a favorable impression. Employers get 100s of resumes every day and they would not have the time to go through every word of your carefully prepared document. They only have 6 to 10 seconds to decide if your resume is shortlisted or sent to the reject pile.

How to prepare the perfect resume:

1. Keep the resume, short and precise. A one-page resume is the best. Write only what is essential, in crisp language without errors, and with perfect grammar. Make sure the resume has the keywords used in the JD. (*Sometimes, automatic systems[3] are used to sort resumes. These programs look for keywords to shortlist.*)
2. Provide a career snapshot that highlights your achievements. Be specific. (Here are some examples: "Increased sales of X by 25 % in 1 year;" "Reduced cost of production by 5% through waste reduction;" "Reduced cost of borrowing by 1%;" Recruited over 125 IT professionals for the overseas project;" " Improved ITR[4] from 8 to 12")
3. Provide an educational snapshot. Highlight your core competencies. Include only the top three qualifications. There is no need to give your grades. Highlight only exceptional achievements like topping the university or getting a national honor.

---

[3]ATS (Automated Screening) – software that screen resumes based on categories set by the company
[4]ITR -Inventory Turnaround Ratio – a good metric for working capital management

4. Avoid unnecessary details like hobbies, membership in clubs, etc. unless these have a direct bearing on the job.
5. Do not use vague and indirect words like "involved in", or "participated in." Use direct, action words: "achieved," "created," "designed," "increased," "reduced," "solved," "led," etc.
6. Avoid cliches and motherhood statements like "team player," "professional," "people person," "action-oriented," "highly skilled," "honest," "man-manager," etc. Let your actions and achievements speak rather than your words.
7. Provide your contact particulars clearly including social media profiles, if active.
8. Your resume is your calling card. It should be easy to read and precise. Do not give false statements. Do not waffle or ramble. Your lies will be found out. A resume should be like a clear photograph—it should reveal your best-identifying features, at a glance.

Cracking the interview

However senior you are, the interview makes all the difference. The interview determines if you get through the door or not. Even when a CEO is hired, out of politeness it may not be called an interview. The euphemism used would be: *Come for a chat…* or *Let's have a drink and we'll talk about it.* But remember that the person who is having the chat is deciding whether you get past the door.

For you, the job seeker, the interview process is critical. You are trying to do three things:

1. Get the interviewer to open the door for you,
2. Decide if you want to enter this door, and finally,
3. Negotiate the terms of entry.

This is the one chance you get. Of course, the employer is also using the interview for exactly these very purposes *but, from their point of view.*

You may expect the interviewers to delve deep into your experience outlined in the resume. They rarely do so unless they suspect that you are fudging an experience detail. The interviewers are checking if you would fit into their company. The question in the interviewer's mind is: *Will he/she fit into our culture? Is he/she cocky? Will we have a problem with this candidate's behavior after joining? Is the energy level a little low?*

Often the decision to hire or not to hire is intuitively taken in the first five minutes of the interview. The rest of the interview is to re-confirm this decision. You must win the trust and confidence of the interviewer in the first five minutes! So, be your best. Dress smartly, be energetic, be truthful and above all, be pleasant.

An interview is a match of wits. The interviewer is trying to assess your fit, in the short time of the interview. You are trying to retrofit yourself into that mold you think the interviewer has in his mind. The interviewer is looking for gaps (areas where you may not fit). You are trying to cover up the gaps that you know exist. In the interview, both will get only a partial and sometimes, incorrect assessment of each other. At the end of the interview, a decision is made on whether you are "ok" or "not ok" for the next round.

Normally, the interview process will check for three different kinds of fit. There may be three different interest groups checking for these different traits.

1. **Technical fit:** Does the candidate have the technical or specific knowledge and skill to do the job? (Generally, a technical person would check this out.)
2. **Personality fit:** Does the candidate have any quirks, or behavioral issues that could hamper performance such as maturity, balance, or emotional weaknesses? (Usually, the HR department would check this.)
3. **Cultural fit:** Do their values align with the company? Would the candidate fit in with the prevailing company culture? (Usually, the CEO or a GM would test this.)

For senior jobs or important entry-level jobs like management trainees, these interviews would be held separately in multiple rounds. Sometimes, there would only be one interview panel where there would be persons tasked with checking out each of the above. Some guidelines for tackling such interviews are given below:

1. In the technical interview, don't try to show that you know more than the interviewer. You may, but the interview is not the place to exhibit your superiority. Remember that the interviewer is also a human, with an ego.
2. If you have a technical gap in your experience profile, it is better, to be honest about it. The interviewer will discover it anyway. It is wiser to assure the interviewer that you are a quick and diligent learner. You can say that in three months you will cover the learning gaps.

(Note: There is no perfect fit for any job. Organizations are looking for candidates who are about 70 % right. If the candidate is a learner, he/she will quickly learn. You, therefore, must convince them that you are a learner.)
3. You may have supplementary knowledge/skills the prospect company doesn't have as of now. You should bring this up in the interview, *subtly*. You could broach the subject that you may have skills/knowledge/experience that the company could find valuable. Let the interviewer take it forward from that point. If it interests them, they will probe further. Be cautious. Do not seem superior or point out that they do not have this skill as of now. Let them figure it out on their own.
4. In the personality and culture interviews, your aim should be to understand the culture of the prospective company. This can be ascertained if you are sensitive. Look for clues from the behavior of the interviewers. Look out for the following:
    - Are there any obvious differences among the persons interviewing you? Is the interview head cutting out the others? This usually gives a clue about the behavioral practices in the company.
    - Is there equal respect and space being given to all? Or do you see the technical or marketing person leading the interview, bossing over the others? Are they giving respect and space to the junior-most member of the panel?
    - Do they treat you with respect? Are you able to see some streak of arrogance or annoyance in the

questioning? Remember, these trends would magnify many times in the actual job situation.
- Do you evidence empathy? If you are struggling with an answer, do they watch you squirm or is there anyone who tries to make you feel comfortable?
- These clues will help you decide if the prospective company is worth joining. A stint in a toxic company is worse than the wait for the right company.

5. Do you sense that the company has a culture that you would not be comfortable with? If so, politely walk out. It is not worth joining an organization to realize that the culture is not suitable for your personality. Some of the toxic cultures are:

   a. **Overwork/over-stressed culture**: Does the company expect 10 to 12 hrs. of work, all days of the week? Is there extreme pressure to perform? Are targets increased incessantly? Here is a true story:
   This is the story of a well-known FMCG MNC. It gave stiff targets for salespersons. They would get midnight calls from supervisors if the targets were slipping. If achieved, there was the customary celebration, but the targets would get revised upward for the next sales period. Everybody was always under pressure. It was considered a sin to leave the office before nine pm on weekdays. Weekends were also intruded upon. Very few lasted more than two years in this organization.

   b. **Abusive culture:** Companies that turn a blind eye towards the regular use of foul language at work.

Those not used to this culture would find it difficult to survive. Imagine getting barraged with choice expletives in meetings every time you miss a target. It may all be posturing and forgotten by the end of the day, but, seriously, would you like to be part of such a company?

c. **Unethical culture:** You are expected to bribe clients/government officials. You are expected to work around the fringes of the law and break them if you can get away.

d. **Gender/caste/creed inequality**: The "casting couch" is also an interview scenario. The candidate always knows by the tone of the interview where it all is going. She/he should guard against this and walk out if the trend is not acceptable.

e. **Culture of fawning:** Employees are expected to act subservient to authority. In many family-owned companies, extreme subservience to owner patriarchs is expected.

During the interview, it is possible to find out some of these cultural issues about the target company. You can find these out by talking to present or ex-employees, reading up on the company, and referring to sites like Glassdoor.

An interview is a two-way process. The job seeker must check if he or she would fit in technically, behaviorally, and culturally. The worst thing to happen would be joining the company and realizing that there are major differences between your values and those prevalent in the organization.

It is better to know this well in advance rather than take up the job and regret the decision. If there are serious value lines that you don't want to cross, it is important that you state them up front.

Facing the interview

Whatever the level, there is always tension in facing an interview. After all, you are trying to sell yourself to a panel. You cannot read the minds of the interviewers. A judgment is being made about you. It is important to face the interview with calmness and equipoise. You must come through as a person of maturity.

Here are a few tips to help you face the interview:

- **Be calm:** After all, it is only an interview, not life and death. This is easier said than done, but, all the same, try to be calm. It makes you come through as mature.
- **Talk less:** Answer the question concisely; don't go on and on. It lands you in a trap of your own making. Remember the adage: it is better to be silent and thought a fool than to open your mouth and convince the listener that you are one.
- **Listen:** Listen, not just with your ears but with your eyes and mind too. Look for non-verbal clues. Watch the body language of the interviewers. Are they leaning forward to hear you—shows that they are interested in what you are saying. Are they looking here and there and probably at their watches? They are probably bored—you may be talking too much.

- **Be honest:** If you don't know something, say so instead of waffling.
- **Don't complain** about your earlier employer, boss, or anything for that matter. Bring positivity into the conversation. Smile. People like those who smile, not whiners.
- **Show energy:** The worst candidate is one who is dull, boring, and displays an absence of energy. An enthusiastic, full-of-life candidate is a joy and often gets hired.
- **Above all, be yourself**. Don't try to be someone else. You are valuable as you are. Your value doesn't increase by pretending to be what you are not.

Finally, I would leave the reader with an interview story to warm your heart and fill it with hope:

A young and bright girl had an image problem. She was a 24-year-old Indian finding her feet in the US. She had completed her MBA from Yale and was interviewing for jobs. She felt she was not smart enough to impress the interview panels. She didn't have the money nor was she able to carry off smart western clothes. They looked very awkward on her. She felt inadequate, compared to other classmates in Brook Brothers suits and silk shirts.

In tears after a blotched interview, she went to the director of career development in her college.

"Look at me," she said, "I went to an interview like this. Everybody is laughing at me." The director understood her predicament.

He asked, "What would you wear for an interview in India?"

"A saree," she answered. "Then wear that for your next interview", suggested the director.

For the next interview, this girl wore a smart silk saree and faced the interview panel with renewed confidence. She got the job. Her name is Indra Nooyi[5], who went on to become the Chairman and CEO of PepsiCo.

Negotiating the terms

Working environment/employee policies

- Is *Work-from-Home* (WFM) encouraged or discouraged? You may wish to clarify your views on the same. Many professionals would like a hybrid work structure.
- *Leave/working hours/work-life balance.* It is good to have clarity on this. it is important to let the organization know that you expect vacation time and would be uncomfortable with extra-long working hours.
- *Office premises*—this is often neglected. It is good to get clarity on where you would be working. Especially if it is a factory, you should know the factory environment in terms of safety, health, cleanliness, and other parameters. It is a good idea to request a factory visit before you commit to joining the company.

Salary Negotiations

- This is the one chance you get to refix your salary. You should look for at least a 25% increase from your current salary. Organizations generally use your current pay to

---
[5] *My Life in Full.* Indra Nooyi, 2021

limit the salary, even though they may have budgeted to pay more. You must resist this move as a job change is one way to get a large jump in salary. You can justify by stating that one of the reasons you are changing the job is to correct the anomaly of getting paid lower than the market.

- All companies have a band across which salaries are fixed for a role. The interviewer's skill is to fit you at the lower end of the band while your attempt must be to fix the salary at the higher end of the band. Don't accept the argument that the company cannot afford your demand. All companies can, if they think you are worth it. Do not get short-changed by a skilled negotiator. Be polite but firm. You will succeed if you are worth it.
- Don't be fooled by the CTC (Cost to Company). This is used as a carrot to draw people into a company. CTC includes all elements like maximum incentives, cash value of earned leave, bonuses, statutory payments like PF/ gratuity, and health cover. Some of these are cashable only in the distant future if you stay in the company long enough. You must also consider the present value of these distant and probable future earnings. Negotiate based on "take-home" salary. You pay your monthly bills with only the cash in hand; all the rest is only good to know.
- Designations are important whether you like it or not. It strengthens the resume. Look for a good designation, but at the same time, don't be fooled by designations. There are large international banks where there are hundreds of VPs while there are more traditional organizations where the VP is the chief operating officer, reporting to a titular

head called the President. The interview is the place to ask for the designation you want. Of course, make sure the job role is in line with the designation.

References

Reference checking is an important step in the recruitment process. This is because no employer wants to take a chance with a candidate. The resume could be false, the interview process could be managed and the only final check is an endorsement from people who know you at work.

Having good references for your work is of paramount importance. Such referees must be nurtured and built carefully throughout your career. Many candidates neglect this during their work and struggle when asked for references by their future employers.

In today's world, this has become even more important. Employers want to know about your affiliations and political leanings and often come near to invading your privacy. And with social media, most people are an open book.

All career aspirants must develop good referees. Some of the steps to do this are:

1. Create friends at work, not enemies. Be good to people so that when asked, they would put in a good word about you.
2. Cultivate good relationships with seniors and bosses. Be in their good books. They would be the persons who would be asked about you.

3. Keep in touch with old bosses and colleagues. Call them occasionally. Keep them appraised of your career progress. Be genuine in your interest in them. A good word from them may be needed.
4. In your specific area of expertise, have a couple of persons who could endorse your work and competence. Keep them updated on your career progress. People forget, so keep reminding them of the great work that you did together. If asked, they would recall what you reminded them of. This would be a great reference for you.
5. Ensure that there are no dark sides to you. These would get found out in a reference check. Cover them up to the best extent you can. If not possible, create explanations that sound reasonable.
6. Social media is important in this day and age. It serves as a reference and is often referred to by employers. Make sure you have a LinkedIn profile and that reflects your personality and job profile. If you have active Facebook, Instagram, or Twitter profiles, make sure these reflect your good side. No employer likes to hire a person with extreme views, who posts vitriolic content, or who is nasty online. Very often a social media post reveals the true you. Make sure it is a personality that a potential employer would find pleasing and valuable.

References are extremely important. It is for you to ensure that whatever your level, there are at least a few who would be willing to vouch for you. Make sure that in every job there are at least two people who would give you a good reference. Here is a useful exercise to check your references:

Exercise 2.1: Building your references

Use the Table 2.2, below. For each of the companies listed in your resume, list two persons who could give you a good reference. Similarly, for each experience in your resume, list names of persons who could vouch for you.

As you do this exercise, you will realize that for some companies/experiences, you currently don't have any credible or good referees. You should then try to build these references. Contact your old bosses and colleagues and re-establish your links. Tell them that you are looking for references. Refresh their memory about you by reaching out and speaking/writing to them. Many would be happy to oblige.

Table 2.2: My References

My References			
Company/ Experience	**Period**	**Referee 1**	**Referee 2**
1. XYZ			
2. ABC			
3. Sales			
4. Product Management			
5. Web Design			

Good references are vital in your job search at all levels. This exercise will help you create these well ahead of your job search.

The first step has been taken. You have started the climb. The rest of the journey will be exciting. But be careful. The path ahead could have hazards that pull you down or slow your pace. But, before that, there is another important topic to discuss. Now that you have got the job, *when is the good time to leave it?*

3

WHEN DO YOU LEAVE A JOB?

*H*ave you heard of A M Naik, the legendary boss of L&T? He didn't get hired at L&T at first because he didn't have the IIT pedigree. He joined another small company and after a few years, he joined L&T as a junior engineer in 1965. And he worked hard.

Many of those who joined with him —IIT engineers—left L&T, to pursue MBA degrees or to jump to senior levels in other engineering companies using the invaluable L&T experience. Naik stayed on and excelled. Through hard work and diligence, he climbed up the ladder, step by step, and became MD in 2003, after 38 years. In 2013, he was ranked among the Best Performing CEOs in the world. He is a legend. He built L&T into one of the finest engineering companies in the world.

Mr. Naik stayed and prospered in the same company. There are equally compelling stories of people who don't stay in a job for more than 5 years and with each job change manage to climb higher up the ladder. They too build impressive careers and leave behind great organizations.

Which is the right path for growth? Is it to stay in the same company and rise steadily or is it better to hop from one position to the next higher position and build a great career? Which is the better strategy? How do you know when to leave the job you are in?

Why leave a job?

People change jobs for a variety of reasons—for increased pay, a better position, unhappiness with the company or boss, etc. Research shows that more people leave firms due to the push factor (*unhappiness with their current company*) rather than a pull factor (*attractiveness of another company*). In this book, we argue that job change must be a strategic choice in the building of a career. It is an integral part of the *Art of the Climb*.

In the eighties, nineties, and earlier, employees started and retired in the same company. At best, they would make one or two job changes in a long career of forty years. All this has changed. Today, people change jobs every four or five years. A report by the Bureau of Labor Statistics, USA[6] shows that the median tenure with a single employer was 4.3 years. This is for all jobs, both white and blue-collar. For managerial and IT jobs, this number is even smaller.

There is no formal study of this kind in India, but search firms and HR professionals concur that this figure is coming down,

---
[6]EMPLOYEE TENURE IN 2022, Bureau of Labor Statistics, US Department of Labor, Sept. 2022

year on year. Apocryphal evidence suggests that the average time spent in a job in India among professions would be five years. But is every job change good? A job change that doesn't advance a career is a wasteful exercise. A correct job change at the right time is integral to career progression.

But before that let us understand a bit more of the nature of a career.

A career—what is that?

As this is a book on careers, it is important to clarify what comes within the definition of a career, at least for this book. This is a book about *corporate careers*. It doesn't include a career of individual excellence, as in the case of an actor, musician, or sportsman. It also does not include an entrepreneurship career (*this is the topic of my earlier book BYOB*[7]). All these are very meaningful and valuable career options. But this book restricts itself to the ups and downs, the challenges, and the strategies needed to climb the *corporate* ladder and enjoy the climb.

A corporate career is a progressive climb starting from the first steps, through the other rungs of the ladders, to whatever height one may reach, in a period of 30 to 40 years. It is a series of climbs (or job positions) in one company, or multiple companies. It is a steady progression in roles, responsibilities, the span of control, and earnings. It involves periods of uncertainty, periods of rapid growth, disappointments, joy, anxiety, and exhilaration.

---

[7] *BYOB- Be Your Own Boss*; C Venugopal, 2021

A career is often a microcosm of life itself with ups and downs. While it offers exhilarating opportunities, the climb is not without the hazards that could pull you down. It is a game of Snakes and Ladders. In the game, for every ladder, there is also a snake waiting to drag you to the bottom of the board. A ladder could be a big one in one firm or a series of smaller ladders in different job environments. A career involves changing jobs across firms or growth within a firm. But first, we must know when to change jobs.

Are you learning and earning?

A job is not just a meal ticket—a place to earn a living. It is your dojo, where you sharpen your skills, learn moves, and practice to perfection while developing endurance and stamina. The present job not just sustains your present but also equips you for the next higher position.

In addition to earning, *learning* in and from your job should be a key takeaway. A job helps you live a good life today. You must also earn for tomorrow and the day after, till retirement and beyond. Just as the battery in a car gains charge while the car is in motion, learning in a job, keeps your battery charged for a longer journey.

If you only earn and *don't learn* on a job, the future is compromised. If you, on the other hand, don't earn enough in a job, you are compromising your present. Therefore, the decision to leave or stay in a job is determined by these two important gains from a job.

The framework given in Figure 3.1 tracks your present job in terms of its earning and learning potential. If you find that a job gives you neither earning nor learning, leave. Do not linger. Many are reluctant to leave their comfort zones and make excuses for not leaving: *things will change; I will get the promotion, next time; after all, there is a recession, so how can we expect the company to revise salaries?* When you see yourself making excuses for your company, it is time to leave.

FIG.3.1 - THE EARNING & LEARNING FRAMEWORK

	HIGH	LOW	
HIGH	STAY	STAY, FOR NOW. (Keep monitoring your learning. Speak to your management about your concerns regarding your earning. Leave, if nothing seems to change.)	L E A R N I N G
LOW	LEAVE, AS SOON AS YOU CAN. (You are in a golden cage. It would get increasingly difficult to leave if you stay too long.)	LEAVE IMMEDIATELY	
	EARNING		

If you are not learning in a job, you must leave. If the salary is too good to give up immediately, wait for the right opportunity to leave. Sometimes, it may even be acceptable to leave for the same level/salary or even lower if the next job promises greater learning. It is the learning that ensures your long-term earning potential. It is your insurance for the future.

How do you know if you are earning or learning enough? You must scope the market and talk to others. Where do you stand, vis a viz your peers from college? Are you better or worse off? Talk to others in the industry. Check the resumes of others in your profession (LinkedIn is a good way to do this). If you were to write your resume, would you be able to genuinely match or better the ones you see on the site?

Similar to how you periodically assess your stock portfolio value to ensure that it retains and grows in value, you must periodically assess your employment value. What is your worth in the job market now? If you were to leave and seek a new job, how much can you expect to be offered by a prospective employer? Are research firms reaching out to you? These are the tips that tell you if your value is increasing or diminishing.

You can also have your own measures or markers to track your learning and earning from your present job. You can use the checklist Table 3.1 to evaluate your learning and earning.

Table 3.1: Are you learning & earning enough?

LEARNING	Y/N	EARNING	Y/N
My job requires me to read and train continuously		My earning is on par with or more than the industry average for my profession	
Every day poses a new challenge in my job		I don't have to think twice to buy something expensive but necessary for me and my family	
I know as much or more than the youngsters who are joining our firm. I am up- to -date.		My company regularly refixes salaries based on industry standards	
My company believes in training me to help me cope with changes in technology		I am saving well for the future. My company has excellent retirement benefits that help me save.	
I have to recertify/ pass exams to update myself professionally, every few years		I have enough money for a vacation with family once a year	

If you have answered yes to most of the questions/statements, then you are earning/learning adequately. If not, it is time to look for a job change. The *Earning and Learning* framework, helps you decide when to leave a job. But there are other considerations for a job change.

Career Pivots

The first job is not always one of choice, but the next one should be. In the 70s and 80s, one stayed and grew in the same company, but not today. In this chapter, we discussed the right timing for leaving a job. The criterion was if you were earning and learning. If yes, you stay and if not, you leave. This is fine. But sometimes, even if you are doing well, you deliberately take a leap of faith into a different career trajectory. Just as a rocket that goes through stages to gain height, a career sometimes benefits from non-linear growth or what is called career pivots. Consider these case studies:

Case Study 1

You are a marketing professional with ten years of experience in (Business to Business) B2B marketing. All your clients are companies (not individual customers) and you deal with the purchasing department of your client to make a sale. You have no experience in dealing with mass markets. You do not understand retail trade. You have never dealt with distributors or C&F agents and you don't understand how BTL (Below the Line) marketing works.

One day, you decide to take a leap and join an FMCG company—a shift from B2B to B2C (Business to Customer) marketing. Your clients now are individual customers. Your sales channel is the distributor-dealer network. It is a completely different ball game from the one you were used to. This is a career pivot.

Case Study 2

You are an engineer and have spent the last 10 years on the production shop floor. You did an online MBA and asked for a change. Your company offers you the job of procurement. Instead of dealing with machines, you will now deal with suppliers. You will have to learn commercial terms and you will have to learn to evaluate suppliers and negotiate with them. This is also a career pivot.

Case Study 3

You are heading the finance function. In meetings, you keep complaining that a specific business unit of the company is not at all focused on the bottom line. You keep talking about how you would run the SBU differently, if given a chance.

One day, the MD takes you on your challenge and promotes you as the head of that business unit with P&L responsibilities. Now, you need to think not as an accountant but as a businessman. This is another example of a career pivot.

Case Study 4

You are a career banker who joined a bank as a probationary officer. After 25 years and 10 transfers, you finally have a choice—to stay on and continue as a banker for another 10 years or to do something new. You decide to take a leap of faith and join an IT company as a head of HR. The environment is new. The average age of the company is 26 as against 46 in the bank. The talk in the canteen is about Java, C++ and the Cloud, which you don't understand. You may struggle for a couple of months but soon you start enjoying it. Every day brings new learning. You have opened new vistas for your career. This is a great example of a career pivot.

Case Study 5

Finally, after 10 years as an employee, you decide to try your hand as an entrepreneur. You no longer have the comfort of a steady income. You must get business and deliver if you want a salary. This is the ultimate career pivot.

A career pivot challenges you. You are in a new and unknown territory. You are out of your comfort zone. It is either sink or swim. This strengthens you mentally and physically. Individuals perform at their best when challenged. Olympic records get broken every time as athletes are focused on only one goal—to challenge the best performer. This dramatically improves performance. Previous records are broken and new records are set. In addition, new ways of excelling in the sport, are discovered as in the case of the Fosbury leap in high jump and many such innovative changes in the styles of playing. Challenge brings out the best in the athlete and the sport. As in sports, this is true in careers as well.

With every pivot in your career, you gain greater confidence. This shows in your body language. With renewed confidence, you perform better. You learn more. You bring the skills learned in one function to the new function and thereby, enhance and improve the function.

A career pivot broadens your outlook. As you move out of a known area and take on something new, you change as a person. In addition to the renewed confidence, you also increase your knowledge. The production engineer who becomes the procurement head brings far greater knowledge of products in use than a procurement officer. This improves performance. Similarly, when a B2B marketing person steps into B2C marketing, he/she brings a new set of tools to navigate the new marketplace. This always makes him or her a better performer.

The broader your perspective, the greater your chance of getting to general managerial and C Level positions. In the case of the banker who pivoted into an HR role in IT, his next move could be as the CEO of an IT services company.

Career pivots take away the boredom of a job. Doing the same job day in and day out can become dull. This results in a lack of enthusiasm that shows on the job. Frequent pivots are one way of keeping the interest and enthusiasm in a career alive. All professionals should look for opportunities to pivot their careers. This is the sure shot way to professional success.

Now that you know how to get a job and when to leave it, it is time to know how to do well in a job. Doing well in a job is not only about achieving the KPIs (Key Performance Indicators) in the KRAs (Key Result Areas). While these are important, career progress requires a different set of skills. The next few chapters will tell you what these are.

Let us continue our climb. One step at a time or is it one rung at a time or one level at a time? How do we know, if indeed, we have moved up? Is our career just meandering along, as if lost on a mountain trail?

A career is sometimes like a maze. You keep going round and round and often find yourself in the same place. You need markers to know if you are progressing—some signs to show that you are moving forward in your career.

The next chapter will help you understand the rungs of the career ladder.

4

THE RUNGS OF THE LADDER

*Y*ou have got that *promotion* but you may still be in the same place in the organizational hierarchy. You may quit a company to join another at *a higher level* only to realize that you are one rung lower in the new company, compared to where you were before. These things happen in careers and job changes. Complex corporate structures could fool you with their many designations, grades, and levels. Therefore, to succeed in your career, you must know the difference between a real elevation and an illusory one.

A career is not a walk up a ramp but a climb on a step ladder with multiple levels. You start at one level, jump to the next, and thereby, move upwards. But does every change take you forward? Not really. The corporate ladder can be confusing.

Here is the story of Anil, a middle management executive:

Anil had joined a well-known manufacturing company. He rose to the JM[8]2 grade in his company with the designation of manager (sales) in five years. After this, Anil's career went into a slump. He was passed for a promotion twice in a row and he decided to leave.

He got a job with Orion Ltd., a larger company in the same city. They offered him the designation of senior manager, a 15% increase in salary, and put him in Grade 4 in their company. Anil was happy, till he joined and started to speak to others.

The new company, Orion had 10 grades with a different designation structure from his present company. The entry-level designation was manager, then senior manager, followed by DGM, GM, SVP, VP, and President.

Anil joined in Grade 4 with the designation of a senior manager. After joining he realized that in the new job, he was one level lower than in his earlier job. The 15% increase was all he had got. Many of his batch who had joined Orion earlier were now DGMs and earning 20% more than him. Within the first six months into the job, Anil was on the lookout for another job. He even sent out feelers to his earlier company that he was open to returning.

This is not an isolated story. Many professionals make job moves, sometimes hastily, only to realize that their frying pan was at least a known one rather than the unknown fire they had landed into. This happens due to a lack of awareness of corporate structures and the organizational pecking order. How do you recognize if a

---

[8]Organizations often have simple grade structures like JM(Junior Management), MM(Middle Management and SM (Senior Management). Each could have subcategories JM1,JM2,JM3, etc.,

jump is indeed a jump, that takes you up the ladder and not one that is masquerading as a snake to pull you down?

Confusing Corporate Structures

Organizations are generally silent on the different layers and levels of the company. This gives them flexibility both for external recruitment, fitment, and internal promotions. Employees want frequent promotions, which the company cannot always give. So, the way out is to give people the comfort of a promotion without actually giving one.

Employees are led to believe that they have got a rise, when, in reality, they may not have. This is achieved by offering visual markers of a *rise*. There are many examples of this: *a larger desk, a bigger cabin, a move to a "senior floor," allowing the use of the senior management toilet* (This is not a joke. In the eighties, companies had different toilets for different levels—the workers, staff, management, and senior management. You knew that you had arrived if you got a cabin with a private toilet.) This kind of promoting is called: *promoting without promoting.*

Another great method of promoting without an actual level of change is through the use of designations. In Chapter 1, we talked of an international bank in the eighties where almost everybody was a Vice President (VP). The joke going around was that they even had VP photocopiers! This bank has scores of managing directors. Sometimes, an India MD would end up reporting to a VP (South Asia), sitting in Singapore. Better designations do not necessarily mean better jobs or higher job levels.

Designations also have a cultural context. Some companies are frugal with designations, while some dole out general managerships to all and sundry. There are also country differences. In India, a director is a very senior person on the board. In US companies, a director is the head of a department. The president of a US company is the ultimate boss. In India, you can have a president reporting to a group president or a COO or CEO. So, if you move from a manager to a senior manager, have you got a level change or have you been fooled into a comfort zone for some time? The only way out of this dilemma for the corporate climber is to understand organizational levels at a deeper level.

Span of Business Control

Your direct responsibility determines your real position in an organization. The board is at the highest level in an organization. They represent major shareholders—the owners of the company. Independent directors on the board are appointed as per government laws, to ensure governance and also to protect the interests of the minority shareholders.

At the operating level, the MD or CEO is the highest functionary, directly responsible for the P&L (Profit and Loss) of a company. His/her position is higher than anybody else's because he/she is answerable to the board for the profits and growth of the company.

At the next level are the business/divisional heads who are responsible for the P&L of the businesses/divisions under them. The heads of functions like marketing, manufacturing, or HR are at the next level, responsible for the management and results of their functional areas. They are, therefore, one level lower in the hierarchy when compared to those who are responsible for the business results—the P&L.

Different organizations have different grade structures. My first company had a grade structure consisting of five levels from the entry-level to that of the CEO. The next one I joined had a 7- grade structure, with non-graded levels above. We knew about the 7 grades and the perks associated with each grade. What happened at the *non-graded* levels was not known to most. Another company had only 3 management levels, (JM, MM, and SM) with three other sub-levels, within each. With such differing structures in organizations, how do you know if a promotion or job change is indeed an elevation?

Most career aspirants are confused with these differing grade structures. Only after joining a company, (as in the case of Anil in our story at the beginning of this chapter), do you realize that you should have been one level higher. It is, therefore, important to understand the real levels of an organization. Each level is also associated with different skill sets and responsibilities.

If you move from a functional role (marketing, purchase, R&D, etc.,) to a P&L role (Business head, SBU head, etc.) then it is real growth. This provides greater learning and prepares you for a CEO role. You can grow along the functional path as well. If you are a technical person, you could grow to be the manufacturing director or the R&D chief. You could grow in finance to be the CFO. These are important positions with commensurate earnings. But, the real power and prestige is when you head the company as the CEO.

Understanding Organisation Levels

The real levels in a company are associated with responsibilities and the span of business control. To know if a jump is indeed a rise, you must ask these questions: Do I have greater responsibilities in this role? Are more people and business functions reporting to me? Am I reporting to a higher-level authority? Are there fewer persons at this level/role than in my previous role?

In reality, there are only five real levels or managerial grade clusters in an organizational hierarchy, starting from the board down to the entry and junior management levels. These levels are based on role, responsibilities, and impact. These levels may be named differently or sometimes not at all. Within each level, there could be several designations or grades. Moving from one such level to the next is *real* growth.

These are described in Table 4.1 below, along with the role attached to each level and typical designations prevailing for the level.

Table 4.1 Real Organisational Levels

Level	Role	Typical Designations
Board	Protection and growth of shareholder wealth; preservation of ethos/values	Director on the Board
Top Management	Strategy, compliance, and growth to meet board objectives	CEO, President, and MD

Senior Management	Operations leadership and management	COO, VP, GM, Business Head, SBU (head); Director (in the US)
Middle Management	Operations management	DGM, HOD, Senior Manager, Group Head
Junior Management	Entry levels – Operations	Management Trainee, Junior Engineer, Associate, etc.

A typical successful career in a large organization would consist of 5 to 10 years in junior management, another 10 to 15 years each in middle and senior management, and 5 to 10 years in top management and the board. This could be in one company or multiple companies. Most don't make it to the top—60 % not going beyond the first two levels, 30% moving to senior management and only 5 to 10% reaching the highest levels of the top management. This is why a corporate hierarchy is often depicted as a pyramid (see Figure. 4.1).

In your career, you must look for opportunities to move from one *real* level (or grade cluster) to the next. This is growth. In formal organizations, moving from one-grade cluster to the next is considered a big jump and is given only after due scrutiny. For example, the promotion of a VP or CEO to the level of an MD is a big rise that is given only after deep evaluation (often by an external consultant). This is because different levels require different skill sets.

Figure 4.1: Real Levels (grade clusters) in organizations

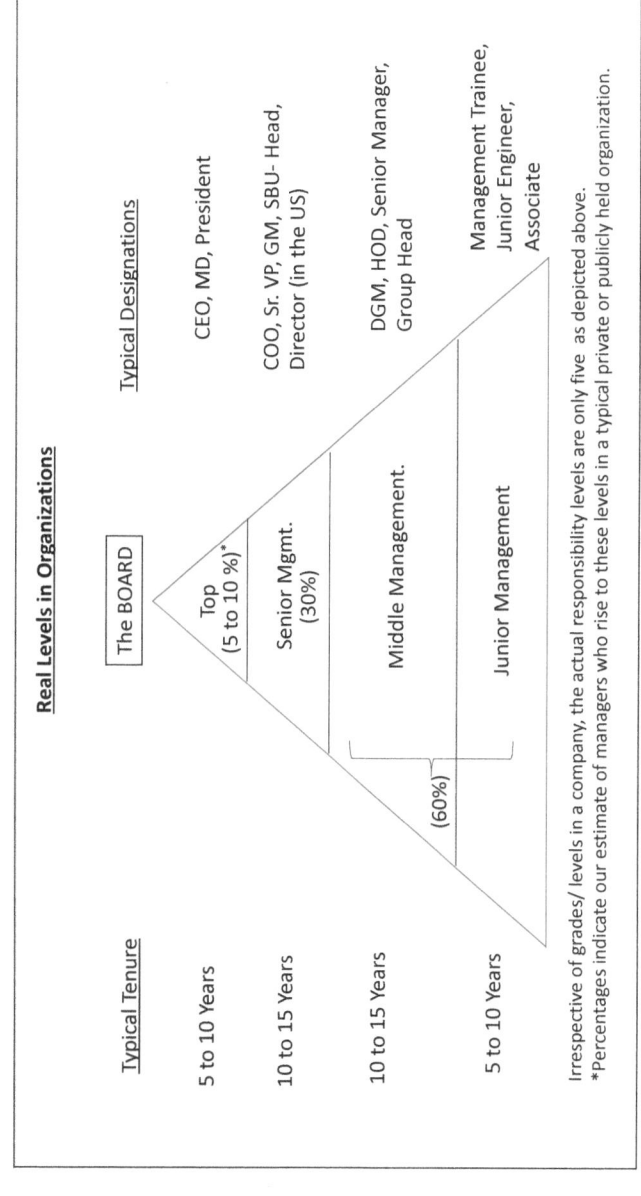

In the first level (junior to middle management), the core requirement is *energy* which is the ability to put in a lot of hard work, enthusiasm, and positivity. The focus is mostly, *near-term*. You are the executing arm of management. You must be able to get the job done.

At the next level, senior management, *strategic thinking* is the core. While you do need to have energy and positivity, the key expectation is your ability to think strategically about the business. The focus should be *middle-term*. You are not the executor but you are responsible for the execution. This means having a larger perspective, better control of emotions, and a loftier vision. Above all the level demands an ability to lead, delegate, motivate, and guide execution teams.

At the top management level, the greatest skill required is *maturity and vision*. The focus is *long-term*. You are responsible for the company's growth in the next decade. You are the custodian of the values of the company. You are responsible to the shareholders through the board. A person who gets promoted to this level is expected to be a leader and a visionary.

Firms look for these qualities when hiring or promoting individuals. For junior/middle management positions, they look for energy. When hiring for senior management positions, employers look for prospective employees with strategic thinking skills. For top management roles, they look for maturity, leadership, and long-term perspective. As a candidate, you must keep this in mind.

Rising steadily in one's career is essential. Just like in the army, each level in an organization is associated with an age and experience profile. For example, with about 10 years of experience and around 35 years of age, you are expected to be in a middle management position. Generally, a fast climber should be in a senior management role by the age of 40. Of course, there is no hard and fast rule, but these are norms that are generally followed. When recruiting for a CEO, a company would look for someone who has grown well and who has at least 10 to 15 years of career ahead of him or her. This gives the person the time span needed to bring about change in the new company.

But, many never make it. The corporate climb is treacherous and there are many known and unknown hazards on the way. The climber must be aware and beware of these hazards. They come in different forms and can pull you down or halt your progress. What are these hazards and can they be overcome? Let's find out in the next section.

HAZARDS OF THE CLIMB

5

DOES YOUR BOSS LIKE YOU?

I had fourteen bosses in a career of thirty years. I didn't get along with at least eight of them. Looking back, with the maturity of age and the distance of time, I realize that, in most cases, *I was to blame for the soured relationships*. It had little to do with performance. The bosses were who they were, I was who I was. It was the combination that made the difference. Mostly, it was my behavior that determined how my boss behaved with me.

There were five or six bosses I liked and who also liked me. My best performance and career growth happened during the tenure of these bosses. This is not surprising because if you are happy and satisfied in the work environment, you produce the best results.

Relationship with Management is the top factor in employees' job satisfaction, as per a report by the international consultant, McKinsey.[9]

The article states, "…*Countless studies show the empirical link between employee satisfaction, customer loyalty, and profitability…*" A boss is critical for both your as well as your company's growth.

For most employees, the immediate boss *is* the company. How the employee experiences the boss determines the employee's feelings towards the company. It does not matter how good the company is. If the immediate boss is unfriendly and unfair, then the company is perceived as unfair and unfriendly. One of the best-recognized employee engagement surveys is the Gallop Q12[10] survey. This survey has just 12 questions that are used to gauge employee engagement in a company. Among the questions, Q4 and Q5 are considered the most indicative of employee satisfaction and performance. These are:

> *Q4: In the last seven days, I have received recognition or praise for doing good work.*
> *Q5: My supervisor seems to care about me as a person.*

Praise and recognition from your boss determine your engagement with the company. Your boss is the most important person for you in the organization. *Art of the Climb* is a lot about the art of managing your boss. Those who learn this early on in their career, do well. Those who don't learn so, neither enjoy nor excel in their careers. It has little to do with your performance or even

---

[9] McKinsey Quarterly, September 2020, The boss factor: making the world a better place through workplace relationships

[10] https://www.gallup.com/workplace/356063/gallup-q12-employee-engagement-survey.aspx

your potential. Most often, your performance in a job depends on your relationship with the boss.

Bosses come in various shapes and sizes. You cannot choose who your boss is going to be. They may come to you because of a promotion—yours or his/hers. They may come because you joined a new firm. A merger of departments or a new re-organization exercise could land you under a specific boss. A situation may arise where someone who was your subordinate till yesterday, becomes your boss. All these situations are common in organizations. Whatever the cause, you must learn to manage the boss you get. The onus is on you. Your career, and most of all, your peace of mind, depends on it. Here are some examples of bosses you may have to deal with:

The toxic boss

I had a boss who stressed me out all the time. He wouldn't smile. Every time he saw me, he had a scowl, which raised my BP levels. I tried to please him, but every attempt was met with contempt or slights, that pushed me down even more. The relationship was so toxic that it was affecting my health. Fortunately, the business head sensed this strained relationship and shifted me away from this boss. It was a relief to get out of the toxic work environment.

While it was horrible when it lasted, this stint with a toxic boss was instructive. It taught me a lot about how to handle toxic, bullying bosses. Learning to deal with such bosses is integral to the *Art of the Climb*. Here are some strategies to neutralize boss bullies:

1. Focus on the task and job at hand. Remember that you are hired by the company to do a job. Do it as well as you can. If there are KPIs to measure performance, keep track of the same and ensure that everybody, including your boss's boss, knows that you have performed. If you perform and there is data to prove it, you are taking away the one legitimate weapon from your boss.
2. Do not allow your boss to emotionally manipulate you. Learn to keep your emotional outbursts in check. Anger, sadness, tears, and frustration are what the toxic boss expects—*the psychological payoff of a bully.* Do not give him/her that. Stay focussed on your work and refrain from getting emotional; *stay rational.* This is difficult, but if you do it, you have taken the power away from your toxic boss.
3. If your boss shouts, respond with silence; talk less. Don't try to explain when the other person is agitated as nothing will register, in any case. Just keep quiet or answer in monosyllables, if needed. Refuse to answer if he/she raises the voice or becomes abusive. Tell the boss calmly, "I can't hear when you shout…" Nothing is more difficult to fight than silence. Your boss won't know what to do.
4. Use body language effectively:
    - When facing the boss don't cringe—brace yourself, pull yourself to your full height, and look the bully in the eye.
    - In a meeting, if the boss is being a bully, turn your body away. Give the message non-verbally, "I don't want anything to do with you or your behavior."

- Don't stand up with your head bowed down when the boss shouts at you. Sit down and face the person *as an equal*.
- If the shouting/verbal abuse gets intolerable, just walk out of the room. There is little the boss can do.
5. Let the others in the organization know about the bad behavior. There may be others facing the same issue. Let the higher-ups know that you are uncomfortable. Never forget that your boss is also a part of the system. You have been hired by the company, not the boss.
6. Finally, if nothing works, then the strategy to implement is GTFO (Get The F*** Out). Staying on in the face of a toxic boss is not good for your career or your health.

In your corporate career, you will meet such bosses. Deal with them with firmness.

The 'nice' boss

The polar opposite of the toxic boss is the nice boss. This is the kind of boss who likes to please everybody. When you are with him/her, they are always on your side. They don't get angry, don't shout, don't oppose—they don't do anything at all. They don't rock the boat and want to just get on with their lives without getting into any controversies.

This kind of boss is also dangerous. Just like a sail needs resistance or a spring needs tension to be effective, a boss also needs to put just the right pressure for you to be effective. A nice boss is often a damp squib boss who will do you no good.

It is easy to be complacent when you have such a boss. Life is cool but a good career is not about being cool. You need to get ahead. A *nice boss* doesn't help you get ahead. Their good behavior is often a cover-up for their lack of confidence to be assertive.

Sometimes, such nice bosses present an opportunity for career advancement. Their "nice" behavior could stem from incompetence. They avoid confrontations, for fear of their innate incompetency being "found out." If you can be the smart deputy, making up for the boss's lack of competence, *you will rise.* The boss will be grateful and ensure that you get good ratings in your appraisals. Everyone knows who is responsible for the results under such a boss. You will get the rewards while not feeling the pressure of performance.

The maverick boss

This is the super-confident, efficient, and competent boss who is envied and often detested by his/her peers. They bring in the results and therefore, continue to wield influence in the company. Such bosses have a fan following. If you happen to be a fan (*and you are under him*), you also get to rise in the organization.

But such bosses can be disastrous for your career. Let me illustrate with a personal story:

My first job was as a management trainee in a large firm. The Divisional Head, the de facto CEO for the division, was a short-statured man who towered over all by his sheer force of personality. Let us call him D. He was the stereotypical maverick boss.

D was my first experience of a super boss, in more ways than one. He was of course right at the top, but more than his position it was his energy and exuberance that made him "super." He cared little for company rules, pushed all opposition (to his ideas) away forcefully, created new business opportunities through maverick thinking and produced extraordinary results.

D, like most maverick bosses, had a cult following. There was the group that was always around him, laughing at his jokes, and regaling in his stories. The followers (which included me) could find no fault in D and sided with him in laughing at and making fun of all other departments and bosses in the company. We, D's followers, were the chosen few who were destined to rise under the charismatic leader. Or so we thought.

While D produced results he also produced enemies in the company—enemies, waiting for the right chance to pull him down. And such an opportunity came.

One day, we found that D was not in the office. This was rare for a workaholic like D. The next day also he wasn't seen in office. When no one had seen or heard of D by the end of the week, rumors started floating around. Some said he was not well. Some said he was on a secret mission for the MD.

After two weeks, the truth started trickling down the grapevine. There was an internal audit inquiry against D. He was asked to stay away from the office and barred from accessing any company documents. His next-in-command, a very docile man who was until now under D's shadow, was made HOD.

Nothing came of the inquiry except that D had overstepped his authority and taken decisions without express clearance from the board. Nothing mala fide was established. But this episode broke D. He was never his swashbuckling self ever again. In six months, he left the organization.

D left but what happened to his coterie afterwards is the real story. They were put under watch and systematically grilled by the auditors. In the organization anybody who was seen as a D's man was ostracised. Their positions were reduced in importance. They were made to feel small in the company. Most of them left the organization in the next few months.

I was too junior to be directly affected by D's inglorious exit. But I was identified as D's man and got the cold shoulder from the new HOD. He was now emboldened by his new status and finally free from the shadow of his erstwhile maverick boss, D. My career in the company, which was going well, suffered. It took another three years for me to catch up and rub off the stigma of being close to the discredited maverick boss.

Be careful of maverick bosses. Be close to them, but also ensure that you do not sour your relationship with the opposite camp.

Your boss—the roaming star

There is an old adage that you should hitch your wagon to a rising star. True, but imagine if the star is not just rising, *but roaming* as well—roaming from one company to another, every few years, always to higher and higher positions. And if you are hitched to *that* wagon, imagine where you would be.

A friend of mine had such a star to hitch his career wagon to. He had joined a company as an assistant marketing manager. His boss, the marketing manager was about ten years older than my friend and took a liking to him. They made a great team together. The boss was mercurial, impulsive, brilliant, and restless. Where his boss was mercurial my friend was systematic and where the boss was impulsive, my friend was balanced and most of all, totally dependable.

The two were so different temperamentally, that many wondered how they got along so well. It was exactly this difference in personalities that made the two gel. One was the perfect foil for the other. My friend's sobriety ensured that his boss's impetuosity was kept in check. His systematic work practices ensured that the boss's mercurial actions were always post-corrected with the necessary back work.

But the boss was restless. In three years, he jumped to another organization as the Director of Marketing. Any guesses on who followed him to the same company as Marketing Manager? My friend, of course. In the next 15 years, the boss moved from one company to another, each change taking him three rungs up the corporate ladder. My friend was always part of the package that the boss took with him to every new company. When the boss retired from his last company as the MD & CEO, it was natural for my friend to inherit that post.

If you can find such a boss, don't let him go, cling on.

There are no bad bosses, only bad subordinates

This chapter started with my history of *bad* bosses. I also gave you a fair warning that *you cannot choose who your boss is going to be*. Now, I am going to debunk all that and tell you that there are no bad bosses, only bad subordinates. So, if I had bad bosses, it was because I was a bad subordinate. Therefore, while you cannot choose *who* your boss will be, you do have a choice of *being the best subordinate*. Your boss's behavior is predicated on how *you* behave.

Here are the five traits you need to develop to get the perfect boss:

1. **Dependability**: Nothing defines a good subordinate better than dependability. If you are a subordinate who can always be relied on to perform, you can rest assured you will have a good boss Your boss should be able to say, "I know he/she will do the job on time. If not, I will be informed, well in advance."
2. **Make the boss look good:** A boss is human just like you. If you make him/her meet their goals and thereby, help them look good in front of *their bosses*, you would have won your boss over for life.
3. **Never outshine your boss:** It is tempting to make yourself look good in front of your boss's boss. In every case, when I look back, I got along famously with my boss's boss, while fighting with my immediate boss. This is a cardinal sin in corporate life and is sure to ruin your career. Let them (your boss's boss) discover the gem that you are, *through your boss's reports* about you rather than through your upstaging the boss, especially in public.

4. **Never argue with your boss:** Dale Carnegie, one of the earliest writers in the area of self-improvement had cautioned us decades ago that[11] *you can never win an argument—you can't because if you lose, you lose it; and if you win, you still lose it.* This is more true in a boss-subordinate relationship than in any other. You don't have to always agree with your boss. State your point of view with facts and without emotion. If your boss continues to argue against your idea, back off. You don't gain anything by defeating him/her in an argument.

5. **Genuinely accept the "boss package":** The boss is who he/she is. You are who you are. Your mission in life is not to change him/her; it is only to survive till you overtake or bypass him/her. The boss may be fat or thin, capable or incapable, friendly, or a sour puss. Accept him/her into your life as such for the brief period that you have to. Just as you don't try to change, fight with, or grow to love the passenger in the next seat on your journey, treat your boss as the passenger in your career journey.

Here are two traits that, if cultivated, would help you manage your bosses very well—*assertiveness* and *adaptability*. On the face of it, they seem to be opposing qualities. How can one be both assertive and adaptable? Here lies the challenge and opportunity.

Assertiveness

This is an important trait. Assertive persons are firm in their resolve and politely stick to this in the face of pressure. They

---

[11] How to Win Friends and Influence People; Dale Carnegie, 1936

do not compromise personal and professional values. This is a character trait.

Adaptability

The quality of being accommodative is being able to get along with different kinds of people and in this case, bosses. An adaptable person can work with all kinds of bosses. Each boss sees him/her as being *on their side*. The boss may be of any of the types described earlier. However, the adaptable employee suitably alters their behavior to suit the style of the boss.

If the quality of adaptability is combined with the quality of assertiveness, you have a powerful combination. The boss-subordinate relationship becomes smooth and stress-free without any compromise on the fundamentals.

***

Let us get on with the journey or shall we say the game? A career is a game of *Snakes and Ladders*, with a difference. In the board game, a throw of the dice decides whether you encounter a snake or a ladder. In a career also, it is chance that throws you an opportunity (*a ladder*) or a hazard (*a snake*). The career game has an additional twist. You don't even know upfront if the square that chance leads you to has a ladder or a snake. You are playing *Snakes and Ladders* blindly. To win in this game, you must learn to transform a potential snake into a ladder.

6

THE INDIAN ROPE TRICK

or HOW TO TURN A SNAKE INTO A LADDER

Mr. Verghese Kurien joined Tata Iron and Steel Company in 1946 as a graduate engineer after completing mechanical engineering. He didn't enjoy the job and was desperate to get out. He applied for a government scholarship to study abroad. There were scholarships in core engineering areas like mechanical, metallurgy, and civil engineering in Germany. But these were in great demand and went to those with political and organizational clout. The only scholarship available for Kurien was to study dairy engineering in Denmark. In his words:[12]

> *"I was sent to study dairy engineering on the only government scholarship left. I cheated a bit though and*

---

[12] https://en.wikipedia.org/wiki/Verghese_Kurien

studied metallurgical and nuclear engineering disciplines likely to be of far greater use to my soon-to-be independent country and, quite frankly, to me than dairying."

Kurien took up the scholarship and earned a Master's degree in Dairy Engineering. He came back to India and worked in the area of dairy development. He was a pioneer and revolutionized dairy management in India by nurturing and developing milk production through cooperative dairy farming. His efforts empowered farmers, uplifted whole villages, and consequently, turned India from a net importer of dairy products to a net exporter and one of the world's leading dairy producers. He is immortalized as the "Milk Man of India."

Fate had dealt him a bad hand—*a snake*. He could have sulked, refused the opportunity, and chugged along in his job. He didn't but took on the challenge of venturing into unknown territory. He turned a *snake* into a glorious career opportunity—*a ladder*. This is the essence of *The Art of the Climb*.

The nature of career progression

Many things can go wrong in a career. You may not get the exact job you wanted, as in the case of Mr. Verghese Kurien. You may get the job but find that you don't like it or you are not good at it. You may get a boss you are not comfortable with. You may have colleagues who are not supportive. You may find that the working conditions of a job are not conducive. Your spouse may not like your job, location, or hours.

Your response to these career events makes the difference between a successful corporate climber and one who falls short in the climb.

Learning this early on in your career will prevent you from going astray. These are only examples. The situation you face may be different and unique. The point to note is that irrespective of the situation, your skill in transforming a hazard into an opportunity makes you a winner.

Let us look at some of these situations.

The wrong start

You may not get that ideal first job. Out of desperation, you join whichever job comes your way. Once in the company, you realize that the position you have is not what you expected. It may be much below what you think you are qualified to do. Your pay may be lower than what others in your peer group are earning. All this leads to dejection, desperation, and untimely exits.

Sometimes, waiting it out is a good strategy. There is a story of a young man who joins a company and realizes that the company is not right for him. He quits and takes up the next job, only to realize that the second job is worse than the first. After a struggle of some five or six years, he re-joins his first company, which actually was alright to begin with. Never forget that grass often looks greener on the other side.

You must give a job time. Don't take hasty or knee-jerk reactions to issues at work. Your position may not be what you expected, but in a couple of years, this anomaly would get corrected. Your salary may be a little lower than your peers. Eventually, these anomalies get corrected. A career, as we keep emphasizing in this book, is a long-distance run.

Do not evaluate your position based on your belief that you are falling short now. What is important is whether you are on the right trajectory or not.

Recall the lesson learned in Chapter 3. A job should be evaluated based on its earning and learning potential. If the present job is giving you the learning, then stay on till you exhaust all you can learn. You may then be able to leapfrog and land a much better job elsewhere.

A step back to leap forward

In a career, sometimes, a step backward may be needed to get ahead. Don't hesitate to take the step. A career should be steered by looking ahead and not by looking at the rearview mirror. A career is like a stock portfolio. It should be evaluated on its potential to give long-term wealth. Just as overreacting to short-term fluctuations is disastrous for your stock portfolio, decisions based on short-term events are not the way to build a great career.

Here is a story that illustrates this:

Amit was a bright IIT engineer who got his dream job in a technical core-engineering role. He was thrilled and started on his job with gusto. He picked up fast and soon was promoted to Project Engineer. In the next four years, he was involved in multiple projects all over the country. But, he yearned for a managerial job and thought an MBA would help him get such a job.

He worked hard for six months, cracked the CAT exam, and got into one of the IIMs. He got top grades and an offer from a leading MNC on the first day of the interview session. The job offer was for their management trainee (MT) program. And here lay the problem.

The MNC made him the offer for the Management Trainee program which was a sure path to general management in five to seven years, if he performed. But, along with Amit, the offer was also made to three others in the class, all of whom were freshers, with no previous experience. Amit had four years of experience under his belt. He felt that he should get a higher start and not be clubbed with other "fresher" MBAs. He asked the company to consider giving him an edge over the others, taking into account his experience.

The MNC was not willing to make an exception. They were recruiting for the entry-level MT position. They assured Amit that the MT program would immensely benefit him. They also assured him that as he progressed in his career, his earlier experience would help him get ahead of others. But, Amit was not convinced. He felt that he was "above" other classmates in terms of age and experience and he was not willing to compromise on his demand for a different starting point. He refused the offer.

Amit joined another company as an Assistant Manager with a higher starting salary than what the MNC was offering. He was thrilled. The other three accepted and joined the MNC.

Ten years into the career, Amit looked back at his career. He had done well. But, not when he compared to his three classmates who had joined the MNC. They were now on the fast track: two of them headed businesses and the third was on an international assignment. At least one of them was a candidate for a board position, in the next five years.

Amit looked back at his folly of not accepting the offer. He had allowed the past to compromise his future. He was dejected and meandered in his career to retire a disgruntled man.

Industry meltdown

Sometimes, a career change could be a disaster. The "sun-rise" industry you enter, overnight becomes a sunset industry due to a combination of market forces and government policy. Here is a story that illustrates how this "snake" was converted into a "ladder."

Alex was a bright finance professional just starting his career after a master's in Finance from London and a few years in traditional banking. Suddenly, there was a global financial crisis and Alex was out of a job at the age of 24. There were no jobs. Alex decided to prepare for the future by educating himself (a good way to manage periods of joblessness). He joined the CFA[13] program.

One year into the program, he joined the MFI[14] industry in Andhra Pradesh, India which had 80% of the MFI companies. It was brought to fame by the Nobel Prize-winning Muhammed Younus[15] and his Grameen Bank. The pay was less, the job far less glamorous than his earlier banking job.

Alex joined the MFI sector hoping to grow and prosper in this new and emerging sector. Then, the industry bombed. Overnight, the government changed rules for MFIs and brought in regulations (ostensibly to protect the marginalized, but probably for political

---

[13]CFA – Chartered Financial Analyst – certification for investment professionals offered by the CFA Institute
[14]Microfinance Industry (MFI).
[15]https://grameenfoundation.org/about-us/leadership/muhammad-yunus

reasons). Small borrowers started defaulting on repayments, and MFI firms started collapsing. The whole industry was in danger of annihilation. Alex was stuck in the meltdown, his career once again in serious jeopardy.

His company was in a mess. Salaries were reduced. Work increased as many key persons jumped ship. The lenders were threatening to call in their loans. The government was breathing down their necks and treating them like loan sharks.

Alex was in a dilemma. He had just joined the industry but the future looked gloomy. He was getting calls from recruiters for traditional finance and banking jobs. What should he do? He decided to stay. He had faith in the fundamentals of the industry. He knew that there was wealth at the bottom of the pyramid[16]. He decided to wait it out and make the best of his situation.

Alex was at the centre of all the action in the MFI industry. Working closely with the MD and CFO, he got involved in the loan restructuring process. As there were very few left in the company, the seniors were grateful to have a youngster do the grunt work.

He also met customers at the grass root level, talked to the demoralized collection staff, liaised with lawyers, and coordinated with government agencies and banks. In two years, by which time the MFI industry was slowly limping back to normalcy, Alex was considered an expert in the MFI sector and was getting invited to government panels to speak on the subject. He also, in the

---

[16]See The Fortune at the Bottom of the Pyramid: Eradicating Poverty Through Profits; Dr.CK Prahalad

meanwhile, completed all three levels of the CFA program. He was just 27 years old.

In another year, Alex was headhunted by an international fund looking to expand in the lucrative area of ESG[17] investing. He had emerged from the career crisis stronger and more resilient.

What are the lessons to be learned?

1. Do not panic and follow the herd. Facing a crisis makes you stronger.
2. Every crisis provides learning opportunities. Make sure you learn from the crisis.
3. No crisis is forever. It will pass. Those who stick on and face the crisis will gain from it. Have faith in your innate abilities. A crisis sharpens your skill unlike any other.
4. Train yourself to be Antifragile[18]. This is the quality of systems to spring back from a collapse stronger and healthier.

The rabbit and the tortoise

Sometimes, as in the apocryphal story, the last man standing is the winner. Here is an illustrative story from my life.

My first job after engineering was in a large multi-divisional firm. We were a batch of eight management trainees. The work was exciting and the learning was good. The group consisted of very smart engineers and MBA graduates, all full of ambition and raring to go.

---
[17] ESG – (Environmental, Social, Governance), areas of importance and relevance
[18] Antifragile:-things that gain from disorder, Nassim Nicholas Taleb, 2012

Among the group was Basu, an engineer, who was a nice and simple guy. While all the others were constantly discussing careers and prospects and who paid how much, Basu was quiet and seemed contented. He was only an average performer but worked hard and seemed grateful that the company had given him a job.

Meanwhile, the batch of MTs was progressing in their careers. But as youngsters, they were in a hurry. Everybody was scanning newspaper advertisements for the next job. Within the first year, two of the initial team had left to join other "better companies." Getting ahead fast was the driving motto. By year three, there were only four left and one of who was lured away by another division of the company. Basu, the quiet humble guy stayed on and seemed contended.

I was getting restless. With every exit from our initial group, my anxiety increased. I applied for every job posting I could find. Most weekends were spent attending interviews, unsuccessfully. After six years, Basu and I were the only ones from the initial batch left.

At the end of the seventh year, I finally managed to get another job. I breathed a sigh of relief. It was not that there was anything wrong with the job, just the restlessness of youth and the feeling that the proverbial grass is greener on the other side. Basu stayed on.

Fast forward to ten more years. I had done well and grown to a general management position. Once on a trip, I bumped into my old friend, Basu, at an airport. I had lost touch with him and was happy to meet up again after more than a decade. "How are you, man? You do look good. Still with the old company?" I asked him

"Yes," he said, " I am the CEO, now. All you smart guys left, leaving the field open to me," he added, with a light-hearted laugh.

Careers, like most other life situations, follow the law of compounding. In the stock market, holding on to humble, non-flashy but steady stocks, over long periods is the secret of great wealth—the power of compounding[19] is at play. In the same way staying on, through thick and thin, in a steady, non-flashy company can sometimes take you to great heights.

What seems like a long python that slowly swallows you may be a long ladder that takes you to the top, albeit slowly.

Other potential career traps

There are many such career traps. You may get a terrible boss who is bent on making your life miserable. You may get into a project with great enthusiasm, only to find that the funds are withdrawn for the project due to changing corporate priorities. You may fail in an assignment: miss out on project deadlines, blotch up on cost estimates, fail to stabilize a plant, face labor issues, land up with incapable subordinates, face mass resignations of the team, etc. Many things could go wrong to jeopardize your career ascent.

Such eventualities are par for the course in a long career. To come through victorious requires an attitude of positivity and hope that you must develop early on.

---

[19] "The first rule of compounding: Never interrupt it unnecessarily" –Charlie Munger

Getting Fired

Nothing can be more devastating than getting fired mid-career. You are sailing along well, have a family, and have piled up mortgages for a home, a car, and whatnot, with EMIs totaling over 60% of your monthly salary and then you lose your job.

You get called to the boss's office. You are told how sorry the company is to let you go. You are left with three months of severance pay. You are devastated. Your self-esteem is affected, you are shocked and terrified about what awaits you.

This is the norm in the US where all employment is *at the will of the management.* India, fortunately, had followed the Japanese model of near-lifetime employment. But, this has changed. Today, you can lose your job any day. It is a reality that you must accept and be prepared for. A book on career must address this issue. It is all a part of the *Art of the Climb.* Here are some strategies to deal with job loss.

- ***It is not life or death***

You need to cultivate the mental attitude that losing a job is not a life-or-death issue. Unless you have this attitude, the event of a job loss will consume you and drive you to depression. But, is it possible to be so stoic about a devastating event like a job loss? Yes! Always remember that many have faced this and have survived. Some have prospered even more after a sacking. Oprah Winfrey, Steve Jobs, and J.K. Rowling are stellar examples of persons who have sprung back brilliantly after being sacked. Closer to home also there are umpteen examples of those who have survived a job loss brilliantly.

You have lost the job, the worst has happened. Now what? You must stay positive and make the best of a bad situation. But, is there anything that you can do to prepare yourself for this eventuality? Let us explore:

- **Be prepared**

All professionals must plan for a possible job loss, *while they are working*. Creating a contingency fund for such an eventuality is part of the planning. Ideally, the fund must be large enough for you to maintain your lifestyle for six months without earnings. This contingency fund should be liquid enough for you to draw on when needed. Saving one month's earnings every year for six years should help you build such a fund. If it is systematically invested in safe instruments, you are protected. Having financial stability is the best insurance for a possible job loss in mid-career.

In addition to financial stability, you must also prepare yourself with alternate sources of income. Having a side gig[20] that you nurture while in a job is a good idea. It could be of various kinds. Some alternative earning streams are (a) teaching, (b) writing, (c) share trading, (d) hobbies (with potential for earnings), and (e) silent partnerships in start-ups with friends. This is just a sample. You must use your creativity and nurture an earnings stream, while working, that can generate income for you, if needed, in the eventuality of a job loss.

---

[20] This is a controversial subject. In recent times leading IT companies are coming down heavily on those doing "moonlighting" (alternate careers while pursuing a career). What is suggested here is that you try to have another income stream as long as it does not compromise your current job.

- *Networking*

It is important to create and maintain a network of well-wishers. You will never know when you would need them. In our careers, we meet hundreds of people. The tragedy is that we do not cultivate such acquaintances into a powerful network of friends.

But, such networks are invaluable, especially in a crisis. It is never too late to start. List out all the people who you studied with and you worked with or came across in your life. Get their contact particulars and re-establish contact. You will be surprised at the number of old contacts who would be be happy to hear from you. Send out a birthday card. Call and talk with no agenda. Such a network would be your invaluable asset.

***

A career is a long journey. You will come across opportunities—ladders that will elevate you. You will also encounter setbacks—the snakes. Your skill is in converting the latter into the former. Then, your career journey becomes enjoyable and fulfilling. But, there are a couple of critical key success factors, that are necessary for career growth and progression. Let us look at a few.

7

RESULTS MATTER

*S*uccess comes to those who deliver results *consistently*. You may be brilliant and you may know a lot, but finally, it is what you *deliver* that makes a difference to your organization and therefore to your career.

The primary business result expected from a commercial organization is profits and growth. This is therefore, the result expected from you also. This is what you are hired to do. Some may have a direct responsibility (KPI) for profits and growth (for example, the CEO, SBU head, etc.). Some may have indirect responsibility for profits (for example, HR, manufacturing, and finance). But, all have this responsibility. Whatever you do, it must be centered toward the organizational goal of profits. Those who deliver on this result, stay and prosper. Those who don't, do not grow in position or wealth and eventually would be marginalized. You may be from a great college, with impeccable degrees; you may be well connected, you may be a thinker and strategist. But all of this is secondary. Delivering results comes first.

Andy Grove is considered one of the greatest managers of all time. As CEO, he converted Intel, a small Silicon Valley start-up, into one of the most valued companies in the world.

He said, "At Intel, it almost doesn't matter what you know. It is what you can do with whatever you know or can acquire and actually accomplish that tends to be valued here."[21]

Achieving Results

Achieving results is a sure-shot way to rise in a career. If in sales, consistently meet or exceed your targets. If in treasury or finance, meet your targets of funds management/cost of borrowing/cash flow goals. If in HR, ensure that recruitment, appraisals, negotiations, etc. are completed well and on time. If in R&D, ensure that your projects are conceived and completed as per agreed timelines. If in production, meet daily and shift-wise targets of production and quality. If in projects, make sure you complete the project on time, within costs, and as per agreed quality standards. If you do this you will rise in the company, if not, you will fall behind. This is the essential mantra for success.

Excuses don't count, only results do. You will face challenges; you could have a resource crunch; you may lack cooperation from other departments or clear direction from seniors; you may face an uncooperative union or there may be governmental hurdles. There are a million reasons for not achieving results. All these don't finally matter. You will be judged on your ability to overcome these difficulties and achieve results.

---

[21] Excerpt from Measure What Matters, John Doerr; Penguin Random House, 2018

Some companies may be more tolerant of mistakes than others. Some may not be as strongly focussed on results like Intel, Google, or Amazon. In such companies, you may last longer. But, finally, in a long career, it is those individuals who produce results that rise. It is not the one who knows a lot, talks a lot, or is charismatic and charming—these are great traits to have, but results supersede all these. These qualities are only a means for achieving corporate results. By themselves, they mean very less for a career.

How to achieve results consistently?

Achieving results is a matter of cultivating the right habits and avoiding bad habits at work. Here is a list of good work habits that must be cultivated in your work life:

1. **Know your (Key Performance Indicators) KPIs** – Do you know what is expected of you, explicitly? Are these converted to specific, measurable, and time-bound numbers? If not create the KPIs yourself as you understand them. Check with your boss if there is alignment between what you think are your KPIs and what he/she expects from you.
2. **Be systematic** – Plan, execute and monitor everything you do. Do not jump into work haphazardly. Every project, however small, must follow this same rigor (subject to #6 below).
3. **Monitor performance** – Get into the habit of self-monitoring your performance. Review your KPIs regularly. Are you achieving them or are you falling short? If you are

falling short, course correct, alert your boss that things are slipping, and seek help. Always keep your eye on the ball.
4. **Declutter your work** – Keep your papers in order. Keep your work desk clean. Regularly review and throw out (or systematically archive) papers. This applies to physical as well as computer files.
5. **Do not procrastinate** – Do things on time, all the time. Do not put off today's work for tomorrow. Procrastination is a bad habit. Replace it with the good habit of timely execution.
6. **Do not fall into the analysis trap** – Analysis is a must, but you must know when to stop the analysis and get down to action. You should not spend all your time debating on the right action and ending up taking no action at all.
7. **Keep a diary** – Never go to a meeting without a notebook and pen. Take notes. Do not trust your memory. Make a "to-do" list and review the same every day.
8. **Know the CTQs (Critical to Quality)** factors for your job. These are the key factors that determine if you have succeeded or not. In some jobs, it may be *timeliness*, in others it may be *cost* or *market share* or *growth* or *customer retention*. Some jobs may hold *zero accidents* as the most desired outcome. Whatever the CTQs (there could be multiple), make sure you achieve these without fail.
9. **Manage time well** – One of the greatest skills to learn early on in a career is time management. Everyone has the same amount of time available. Achievers know to use this time valuably. The essence of time management is (a) prioritizing (knowing what is important and when), (b) allocating (dividing available time among the tasks),

(c) focussing (doing one thing at a time and not getting distracted while doing it), and (d) first time right (do things well with focus so that you don't have to redo and waste time).

Make a habit of *always achieving results*. It must be a habit that is cultivated early on in the career. Do not slack. However humble the result expected is, *make sure you achieve it*. Your boss may have asked you to do a small task, say, make a call, prepare an agenda for a meeting, arrange for whiteboard markers that actually work for the meeting, etc.—however small—make sure you get it done.

You must create a reputation—*this guy is reliable and he/she will always get the job done*. Such a reputation is a sure-shot mantra for organizational growth.

Everybody likes the person who always delivers.

Here is a model to consistently achieve results:

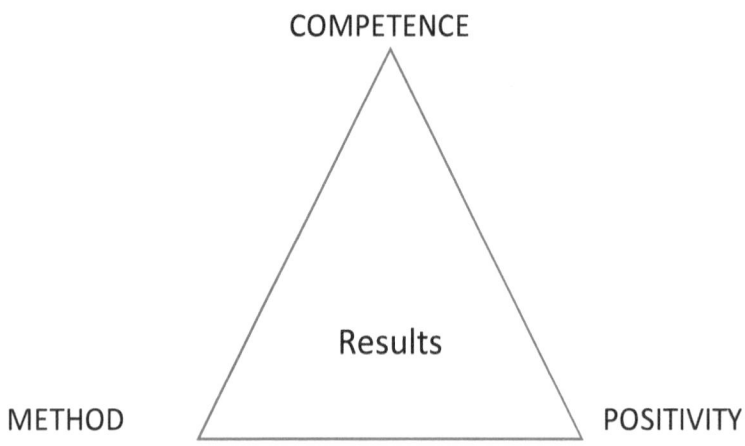

Competence

You must excel in both knowledge and skill in your area of expertise. Knowledge is a deep understanding of your area of work. Skill is the speed and dexterity with which you complete the work. Ask yourself this question, "Are you the go-to person for anybody who has a problem in your area of work? If you can confidently say YES, then you are competent. Build such a reputation in your company.

Method

You may be competent, but to be effective you also need to be efficient. This requires the right method. Planning, allocating time/resources, reviewing, and measuring work output are all part of *the method*. This is not difficult; it just needs practice. Instead of doing things haphazardly, right from the start, learn to work methodically. You will produce results far exceeding your competence. Developing the right habits of working is integral to your succeeding in a career.

Here is an example of a method for consistently achieving results:

O-KRs

A technique for consistently achieving results is the O-KR (Objectives–Key Results) method[22] followed by leading companies like Intel, Google, and Facebook. It is a substantially improved version of the MBO (Management By Objectives) a technique introduced by Peter Drucker in 1954 and further

---

[22]*Measure What Matters – OKRs - The Simple Idea That Drives 10X Growth*; John Doerr, 2018

developed by management theoreticians like Douglas McGregor and John Humble, in the sixties.

In this technique for every goal, the objective is stated clearly in measurable terms with timelines. This is broken down into three or four measurable results with timelines, which if achieved, the objective would be achieved.

Given in Figure 7.1 is an example of O-KRs for a company. This cascades down to all operating levels in the company. O-KRs are developed with all concerned participating in the process. These are then monitored regularly. All systems including appraisal and remuneration are aligned to these OKRs and their achievement.

The O-KR system can be used for the achievement of personal goals as well. Life goals related to health, learning, and earning can all be managed and monitored successfully using the O-KR method.

Figure 7.1 An example of management by O-KRs

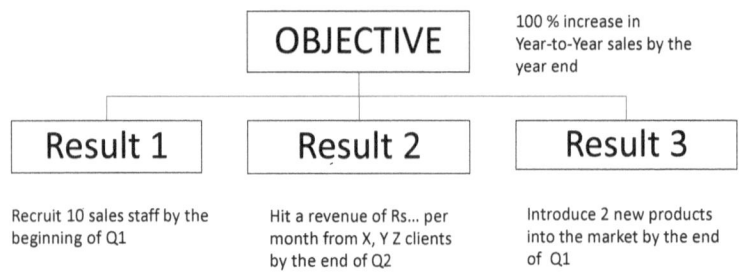

Note: The objective has been broken down to three specific results the teams can work towards. The results are specific, and time bound. These are monitored by the supervisor and corrective action taken, in case of negative deviation.

The OKR technique is one example of a method to achieve results. Several other techniques produce results. Some of these are:

1. Convert each of your objectives into "tasks to be completed." Write these down in a checklist or "to-do" list. Review at the end of each day and score off with a red pen all completed tasks. Make sure that each day's task is completed without fail. This looks mundane, but the impact of this habit can be life-changing. A great book to read on the subject is *The Checklist Manifesto* by Atul Gawande.
2. Manage your time. Most of us keep putting things off till they become a crisis. The 4-Quadrant method of prioritization is a method to break this habit. This is well described in the classic written by Steven Covey[23].
3. Sharing and Delegating: In an organization results are a team effort. Often managers keep things close to the chest—not sharing, not delegating – leading to stress and non-achievement of results. Learning early on the method of delegating work makes the difference between successful and unsuccessful managers.

Positivity

It is natural to feel dejected when things go wrong, as they will sometimes. However, if you stay positive and calm in the face of difficulties, you will be better equipped to face problems and produce results. If you are positive in your outlook, not only will you succeed but you will also create an eco-system around you

---

[23] *The 7 Habits of Highly Effective People,* Steven R Covey, 2000

that is positive. A calm, cool, mature, and rational mind is the best tool to produce consistent results.

Results 360°

Achieving results is important for career growth. Many executives on the fast track know this and are often ruthless in achieving results and even *grabbing* results from others to advance their careers. Such people may rise but eventually get found out. Such people also are not liked and this affects their careers.

A good leader not only achieves his/her results **but also enables others to achieve their results.** *"Others"* refer to not only subordinates but also peers and bosses, hence the coinage Results 360° (an adaptation of the 360° appraisal)[24] concept. Let us see how it works:

Subordinates: Let your juniors see you as a person who helps them win. If you see someone struggling with a problem, offer help without making it known to all and sundry. Let your junior get the credit for a victory and you take the blame for any failure. This requires great maturity and large-heartedness. Dr. Abdul Kalam was such a boss and the people who worked with him talk of this characteristic in glowing terms.

Peers: With juniors it is easy, but what about with peers? Should you help them also achieve results? Are they not your competitors, after all? Not really! Helping peers achieve results and win is a powerful strategy for career advancement.

---

[24]In the 360° appraisals, an individual is appraised by not only the boss but by peers and subordinates as well. This provides the individual with an all-around view of himself. This appraisal is used by organizations as a development tool.

Peers could cut across departments. Business results come from all departments working in tandem. If you can rise above departmental rivalries and help other departments also excel, you will be seen as a person who is fit for senior leadership. In addition, the other person or the other departments will never forget and you will forever have allies and friends. In a long career, believe me, you need more friends than enemies. Such acts are not hidden from the organization. Everyone including your bosses will know that you helped. This prepares you for leadership.

Bosses: When you help your boss look good in front of their boss, you have a friend for life. Nothing endears you more to a boss than your helping him or her achieve *their* results. As we have repeated earlier in this book, your boss is also human and another employee like you. If you go out of your way and help him or her succeed, they will see you as the most promising resource, deserving growth.

Achieving results is paramount to building a great career. But there are times when despite achieving goals and getting the expected results, your career seems to be going nowhere. You are a great performer but when it comes to promotions, you are overlooked. You are frustrated. You will wonder what is wrong. Despite meeting all my targets, why am I not considered for senior leadership? What am I doing wrong?

There is something even more important than results to succeed in a career. Read on…

8

BEHAVIOR MATTERS EVEN MORE

When I look back at my long career, I can recall many instances when an insensitive remark made by me or a thoughtless action spoiled a relationship. Later on, I regretted my action, but, by then, it was too late. There is a truism to keep in mind: *you cannot talk yourself out of a situation that you have behaved yourself into!*

You are judged by the way you talk, act, write, and transact with the world. Even non-verbal actions, such as *gestures*, *smiles* (or lack of smile), and *mannerisms*, define you. Brilliant careers are often halted or seriously impaired by bad behavior.

Your behavior determines your ability to influence and lead. A career is a team game. You win or lose together. Some rise to the top to be captain, many don't. Individual brilliance is needed, but what wins the game is collective brilliance. Those who can facilitate and foster teamwork climb the corporate ladder. Those who don't, stop midway. Often, your behavior, as a peer or a boss, facilitates or impairs your ability to lead.

Whether you are a management trainee, a mid-level manager, or even a C-suite aspirant, your behavior could land you in a mess. Here are some examples to illustrate:

Wilfred was a capable manager, except when he got angry. In such a situation, it was better to avoid him. One day, he had to make a presentation in an hour but the OS decided to upgrade just then. The upgrade went on and on and on. Wilfred tried to kill the process, but the icon continued to go round and round, and Wilfred was getting angrier and angrier, till finally in a fit, he flung the machine out of the window. Wilfred did not grow beyond being a departmental manager in his company.

Sheila and Daisy were both brilliant. One qualified for the IPS exam and grew to the level of a DIG of police. Daisy qualified as an IAS officer and became a district collector. Sheila and Daisy couldn't stand each other. It started way back when they were both civil services aspirants. The rivalry continued throughout their careers. The animosity went to the extent that Daisy had to stay clear of Sheila in meetings, which as state officers, both had to attend. Sheila just couldn't control her tongue as far as Daisy was concerned. The final straw was when Daisy posted some nasty pictures of Sheila on her social media handle. Sheila retaliated with full vigor through the press.

The whole country was watching the catfight with amusement and glee. When the spats between the illustrious ladies started getting played on national channels, the powers that be decided that "enough was enough". Within a day, both the promising civil services officers were suspended and sent home on long leave. One wonders how extremely bright and capable people behave like teenagers. That is the nature of behavior bloops; they drag you down no matter how great you are.

We have all heard of President Clinton and his proclivity for young interns. For all his sagacity, intelligence, charm, and maturity, when it came to women, he was worse than a teenager. Mani Shankar Aiyer, an otherwise smart man, couldn't control his tongue when it came to Prime Minister, Modi. The former went into political oblivion and the latter used every faux pas to full advantage. These are well-known examples of behaviors affecting political careers. The same is true of corporate careers as well.

All corporate climbers must learn this lesson early: *managing one's behavior is key to managing one's career.*

Managing Behavior

If you look back at your career, I am sure you will recall instances of unthoughtful or impulsive actions that have cost you dearly. *I do* and I also often wish I had the help of a career coach who would have warned me to change my ways. One of the purposes of this chapter is to be that coach who holds a mirror up to you making you aware of the behaviors that may be dragging you down.

How do you recognize such behavioral patterns? One way is to paint word pictures of stereotypes you would have encountered. This brings to the surface the behavior. You may identify with the stereotype and get that *ah-ha* moment that helps you change. Here is an exercise to help you:

Exercise 8.1: Identify the Stereotype

Please go through the description of each of these stereotypes. Do you see them in your workplace? Do *you* fit into any of these yourself? Internal reflection is the first step to change. Often we are not aware of how we project ourselves to others. These stereotypes may prompt you to wonder: "*Am I like that? God, I never realized…*" This realization is the first step to change.

The Angry Young Man (woman)

This guy (or gal) has a short fuse. The slightest provocation is enough to send him/her into a fit of anger. It could be a disagreement, a mistake, or something silly such as an unclean bathroom, tea spilled onto a saucer, the color of somebody's dress, or a spelling mistake in a document. With subordinates, the anger erupts as a tongue-lashing; with peers, shouting and walking off; and with superiors, sulking and non-cooperation. People tread softly in the presence of such persons.

If you encounter such a person in your workplace, beware, be warned, and take precautions. Try to find out their triggers and pet peeves. It could be something quite silly, for example, a *state of cleanliness, typos in memos, political likes/dislikes, food habits (veg or non-veg), environment or gender issues.* The list is long. Once you find the trigger, ensure you don't press it!

The Pessimist

Nothing is more irritating than an eternal pessimist. This person always sees the worst of any situation. In every project discussion, he/she would tell you three reasons why it would fail. For such people, the policies of the government/company are always wrong. He/she is sure that people will make mistakes, the food in the canteen will be bad, the fourth wave of the pandemic will come and be worse than the third and so on.

Such persons have something negative to say about everything. They dampen the mood, always. There is an old management book called the *Zapp! The Lightning of Empowerment*[25]. It says there are persons who energize (*Zapp*) with positivity. In contrast, there are other negative persons who *sap* enthusiasm and energy with his negativity. A *pessimist* is the classic manifestation of the *sapper*.

If you have such a person in your company, as a team member or a boss, stay away. Such negativity is contagious. If you, perchance, are a pessimist yourself, then there is a need for some serious introspection. What is the reason for this attitude? Is it to do with some past disappointment? Whatever the reason you must force yourself to snap out of it. The moment you sense that you are behaving in a pessimistic manner put a brake on those negative thoughts. List five positive factors that are positive to the issue. In this manner, use the power of your will to fight the negativity.

---

[25] *Zaap: The Lightning of Empowerment*, William Byham and Jeff Cox, 1991

The Sycophant

This person sucks up to authority, always agreeing, and nodding their heads irrespective of what they believe. They never reveal their mind, wait to see how the wind blows and then set their sails accordingly. You will meet many such people in your career. Early on in my career, I had a colleague who was such a sycophant that he even named his son after the patriarch (father of the MD) of the company. He also made it a point to remind the owner MD of this fact on every occasion. This guy was among the first to be let go on one of the cost-cutting drives of the company.

Normally, such people get found out and are marginalized. Organizations recognize the damage that such persons can do. While bosses love to hear good things about themselves, they also realize (or at least should) that people who chant "*Yes, Master*" always are not the best for organizational growth and prosperity.

The Fence-Sitter

These are the type of persons who will never commit to a course of action, leaving things vague and simply waiting for you to succeed or fail. If you succeed, they will say, "See, I supported you." If you fail, they will disown you. They are so risk averse that they would rather postpone a decision rather than take a *wrong decision*.

I had a boss who was such a *fence sitter*. You take a proposal to him and he would return the same after a few days with the remark saying, "Need greater details, please." If you send in a detailed proposal again after a few days, you would get the same returned with a scribble, "A high-level summary, please…I don't have all day!" This back and forth would go on till out of frustration you would either abandon the proposal or go ahead without specific approval. If things turned out well, he would be the one to brief the MD and if not, he would be the first to question how actions are taken without approval.

The Know-It-All

He/she knows it all. They have been *there* and *done that*. In any discussion, this person always has the answer: "Oh, I know, in my old company we faced a similar situation…" or "…Oh that, I know, in this article I read…" He knows it all. Every instance is labelled or pigeonholed into an existing framework by this person. After a point, it gets irritating.

There was a smart youngster in my earlier company who behaved in this manner. He was bright and knew a lot, but the moment he started, the rest of the group would roll their eyes, "Not again." After a while, the boss had to intervene if this guy started his comments.

"Not you," he would say, "Other than Mr. Smart Aleck, does anyone have anything to say?" This would get peals of laughter from everybody else. The poor guy didn't know if he was being praised or ticked off. The tragedy was that for a long time, he believed the former and carried on.

The Joker

This person revels in his sense of humor. He cannot avoid a witty repartee in meetings or conversations. You will ask, "What is wrong, isn't this a good trait? It lightens the mood and counters the stress in meetings." You are right. It is a good trait but only up to a limit. But, beyond this limit, it is an irritating habit.

The problem is that witty people sometimes get carried over by their wit. For them, everything, every situation, and every person is the subject of their wit. They are compulsive jokers. They are so caught up with the need to be funny that they are insensitive to the fact that many not enjoy the joke.

This is just a sample of the negative behaviors that impede career progress. Learn to recognize them in yourself and step by step overcome them. This will go a long way in speeding up your career journey.

Positive Behaviors

In contrast to the negative positive behaviors facilitate career growth and success. If you know what these are and systematically make them a part of you, your career will accelerate. These are a few good habits to pursue:

Smile: A smile is a powerful career elevator. Dale Carnegie in his iconic book, *How to Win Friends and Influence People*, gives 30 principles of effectiveness. The 5th principle is: *Put a smile on your face, it really can make a difference.*

Praise: Everybody loves to hear good things about themselves—everybody, from the lowliest to the mightiest. Don't lie, but look for an opportunity to praise and you will win over people. Praise must be genuine not contrived or false. People are sensitive to false praise. Sincerely look for opportunities to complement another person. This is real praise. There is a thin line between false praise and genuine praise. If you find this line, you will have found the magic of getting great bosses, wonderful subordinates, and cooperative colleagues.

Listen: When in a conversation, focus on what is being said and listen. Not just with your ears, but with your whole being. Be with the person and focus on both verbal and non-verbal messages. Often, silence also communicates. Pay attention to what is not said. Giving your undivided attention is the greatest respect you can give another person. The greatest disrespect is not listening. If you treat the person you are interacting with, as the most important person to you, you will have won over the person. This is the secret of the success of many great leaders.

Be Proactive

In a job, you can choose to act, ignore or criticize others for acting. You are proactive if you act. This is the sure-shot way to get noticed and move up the ladder. The easier and safer option is to not act and the nastier option is to criticize others who choose to act. Being proactive is of the essence of the Art of the Climb.

These habits, or action modes, shape character and if made a part of behavior would boost your career trajectory. Never forget the core lesson of this chapter: no one can read your mind, they experience you through your overt behavior. Changing your behavior will change how others perceive and react to you.

Follow the ethical path

A career is a long journey. As you grow in the company, your influence also grows. Your actions or in-actions will impact not only your company but the larger society as well. You can do good or bad with this power; the choice is yours. You also have the advantage of knowledge asymmetry where you know much more than the persons who would be impacted by your products or services. You can choose to selectively disseminate this knowledge and no one would know. Use this knowledge and power wisely.

Imagine that you are a senior person in a pharma company introducing new drugs. You have all the information on the drug trials—the negative as well as the positive. The public who would use your drugs does not have all the information. In such a case, would you suppress the negatives to protect your company's interest? What prevents you from doing so? Why is it that some CEOs cover up the negatives, while some don't? This is *ethics*.

Poor ethical practices of companies result in company and career disasters and there are examples of this all around us. Theranos Inc, Enron Corporation, Satyam Computer Services, and Bernie Madoff, the stockbroker are all examples of corporate fraud carried out by professionals. The CEOs of these companies did these to boost company profits but they were caught and have paid the price.

Martin Luther King Jr. said these important words: *"The arc of the moral universe is long, but it bends toward justice."* He said it in the context of nations, but it is equally true at the individual level also. If you do something wrong, you may get away for a while, but you will eventually get found out. You will pay the price.

Therefore, an important aspect of the *Art of the Climb*, is to stay in the straight and narrow path that is ethical. If you deviate, you will eventually fall down the precipice, much like many before you have.

You have come a long way. You have steadily climbed the corporate ladder. You have become aware of dangerous habits and are working towards overcoming them. You have cultivated good habits and methods. You have been delivering results consistently. You are looking for greater things. You are ready to challenge the summit.

But, what headwinds would you face? How should you prepare for the final ascent?

THE FINAL ASCENT

9

STRESS: THE CAREER KILLER

$\mathcal{H}$ave you experienced a feeling of being powerless at work? It may be in the middle of a project that is going nowhere; it could be at the prospect of meeting your boss for an appraisal; it may be in handling a difficult subordinate; it could be a client who wants to cancel a contract; or a supplier who refuses to supply unless the earlier bill is cleared. It could be a decision that has gone horribly wrong. It could be one of a million things that you face at work every day.

You freeze. You don't know what to do. You feel the heat even under the cool air conditioning of your office. Your neck muscles tense. Your heart rate goes up. Your palms sweat. You cannot think straight. You snap at everyone. Your mind is racing and the internal dialogue is non-stop, painting a zillion worst-case scenarios. A splitting headache is on the way.

This is stress, the career killer. Probably more careers have been halted by stress than any by other reason. But, *what is stress?*

How is it caused? Is it all bad? Can it be turned into a good thing? Learning to manage stress early on in your career is an essential element of the *Art of The Climb*.

What is Stress?

Stress is a primitive survival response of all creatures to the fear of danger. It energizes the body to a "fight or flight" reaction. In all sentient creatures this fear, or fear response, is in the presence of actual danger. However, man has imagination. Even without real danger, man imagines or anticipates danger and the body responds in the same manner as in the case of actual danger.

The body's response to actual or imagined danger is the same: faster breath, accelerated heartbeat, and higher BP, triggered by hormones like adrenaline and cortisol. These hormones increase the sugar levels in the body for energy, rush blood to the limbs to provide more oxygen to the muscles and tense the muscles to strike or run. All of this is aimed at helping us fight the danger or run away from it. When the danger recedes, these hormones are supposed to return to normal levels. Here lies the problem. In the case of man, we imagine and magnify problems even if none may exist. This creates the same stress response as in the case of *real* danger.

When we imagine danger and live in constant fear, our hormones at elevated levels continue to course in our bodies doing their job. The mechanism that was designed to protect us now kills us slowly by keeping blood pressure at elevated levels, increasing blood sugar levels, and thrashing our immune system. The diseases that follow (hypertension, diabetes, high cholesterol, spondylitis, etc.) are quaintly known as lifestyle diseases.

Stress makes you ineffective at work. Your decision-making is no longer rational. The people around you are confused and cannot recognize the new you. "Don't go to the boss, he is in his usual bad mood," is the talk in the office. Your bosses get wind of your mood swings very soon and start doubting your suitability for senior roles. Stress can also shorten your career, as you may drop dead! Learning to cope with stress is an essential first step in career management.

Is stress all bad?

All stress is not bad. Stress is what enables an athlete to smash a record. When a student excels in an exam, stress is at play. When a doctor does three continuous shifts to attend to patients in an emergency, it is stress that provides the impetus. When a team achieves an impossible task, it is collective stress that enables the breakthrough. There is *good stress* and *bad stress*.

Peter Senge, in his imitable book, *The Fifth Discipline*[26], introduces the concept of *creative tension* which is the *good stress* we speak of in this book. The image below illustrates the concept:

---

[26] *The Fifth Discipline: The Art & Practice of the Learning Organization*, Peter Singe, 1990, 2006

Art of the Climb

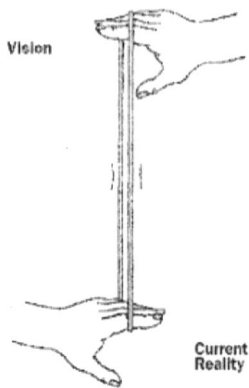

The rubber band between the hands is under tension (stress). This tension (good stress) keeps the band, taut and ready to spring. If it were loose, it would fall limp and if stretched too tight (bad stress) the rubber band would snap. A bow needs tension (stress) to dislodge the arrow but too much of it can snap the bow.

The same is true of a wind-up watch spring. If is not wound, there is no tension and the watch doesn't work. If it is wound too tight, the spring would break. The right amount of stress is needed. This is *good stress*. Excessive stress makes you dysfunctional and this is *bad stress* (See Table 9.1)

Table 9.1: Good stress and bad stress

	Good Stress	**Bad Stress**
1.	Anticipation of winning an order	Fear of losing an order
2.	The excitement of a new launch	Worrying about the failure of the launch
3.	Working hard to meet the target	Panic over not meeting the target

4.	Challenging the boss's decision when you have a different view	Saying "yes" to the boss when you internally disagree
5.	Strategizing to make up for lost market share	Shouting at the team when there is a loss in market share
6	Problem-solving mode	Problem denial mode
7	Facing a difficult decision	Avoiding a difficult decision
8	Searching for a job when you lose one	Worrying and feeling depressed when you lose a job

As you can see, in each of the above situations, there is a positive way to address the issue that leads to creative tension (good stress) and a negative way that leads to bad stress.

External events like winning/losing an order, tight work schedules, workplace differences, problems, or even a job loss will happen in everyone's career. The mental mode with which these are handled makes the difference between a winner and a loser. A positive energizing mental mode is *good stress*; a negative debilitating mental mode is *bad stress*.

Understanding Stress

The key to managing stress lies in understanding its nature. Once understood, stress can be managed. Here are some basic facts about stress:

1. Stress is *your* mind and body's reaction to a real or imaginary incident or issue.

2. Stress is almost always caused by *internal* rather than *external* factors. This means that two individuals will feel different levels of stress when faced with the same external stress-creating factors.

Therefore, if you have to fight stress, you have to work on yourself. You have to develop the capability of managing your reactions to work events. In a long career, you will face all kinds of issues—bad bosses, bad teams or subordinates, failing products, missed timelines, adverse government policies, cash flow issues, labor problems, accidents, etc.

In each of the events described above, you have the choice to give in to stress by shouting, sulking, and getting angry, or to deal with the situation maturely and effectively. How you react determines whether you will grow in your career or get side-lined as one who is not in control. You view events that happen through your filters (See Figure 9.1). These filters are a result of your state of mind and your emotions. Each person sees the same situation but reacts differently.

Figure 9.1 Filtered Perception

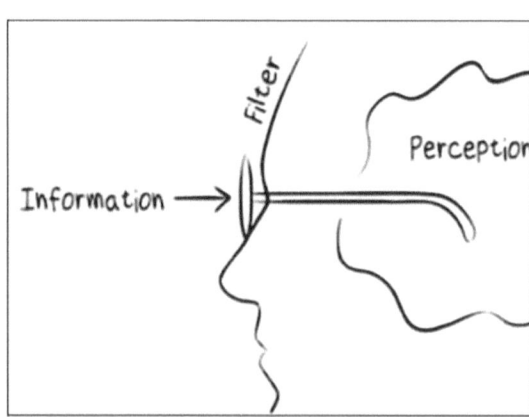

The Cool Cats

Haven't you come across colleagues/subordinates/managers at work who are "cool cats?" Such people never seem to get agitated. The boss may shout, the machine may break down, sales may drop, and targets may not be met. Everybody is screaming and shouting and running here and there. But this person does not display any signs of agitation but carries on with their work, trying to solve the issue calmly. Let me illustrate this with a story.

I was working in a company that had factory operations. One day, in the middle of a meeting, a supervisor rushes into the meeting and whispers something to the president who was conducting the meeting. The president immediately stopped the meeting and called a few of us seniors into his room.

"There has been a serious accident in our plant. One of the workers has been electrocuted and has been rushed to the hospital. It doesn't look good. The employee may die," he informed us. We were all shocked.

The plant head just collapsed into his chair, "Oh God! What do we do?" He was directly responsible and he was paralysed into non-action.

"It is all because of the faulty switch gear that I warned about," said the VP-Engineering.

"No one follows safety. This was bound to happen," wailed the head of the TQM department.

Everybody was shocked and had some explanation for what happened. There was total confusion and inaction. Everybody was frozen.

Then our President got up from his chair and said in a calm, but stern manner, "Shut up, all of you, I am responsible for what happened, and will take full responsibility for it. So, all of you just sit down and focus on the next steps."

He quickly formed three teams. To the first team, he said, "Go to the hospital, take money with you, and do whatever it takes to make sure the necessary steps are taken." To the next team, he gave the task of informing and assisting the family of the victim. The third team was tasked with handling the labor department and complying with all the statutory issues related to a factory accident.

The President kept his cool and took action. Others were frozen to inaction. This is an example of paralysis caused by a stressful event. Panic does not help; it only aggravates. One must be able to think rationally amid a crisis. This is a characteristic that gets noticed and rewarded in organizations.

Emotions are at the root of stress

Stress is caused by our *out-of-control* emotions. There are six core categories of emotions:
1. Fear
2. Anger
3. Sadness
4. Shame
5. Disgust
6. Jealousy

Most of these are a result of our deep-rooted beliefs, our feelings of self-worth, our conditioning, and our childhood traumas. As adults, we must revisit each of these and re-evaluate their relevance today.

A work event triggers the emotion. This emotion triggers another. We act under the influence and do something stupid, which we regret instantly. But the deed is done and cannot be undone. This is how the circle of emotion works and destroys careers.

Let us understand with an example:

You are working on a pitch at night for an important client meeting tomorrow to clinch an order. You are struggling to make the right pitch. You get a few thoughts[27] in your mind:

> *What if I screw up and we lose this order?*
>
> *I will not meet my target* (fear). *My boss will surely give me a poor appraisal. I will not get that promotion this year also* (sadness).
>
> *I am doomed. I am useless* (shame). *Anil's team will meet their targets as they always do* (jealousy).

As a result of this flurry of emotions, you close the presentation *without saving*. Then...

> *Damn, what an idiot! Damn, damn. 2 hours of work lost!*

You become angry and bang the table and topple the glass of water all over the keyboard.

---

[27] Such thoughts are known as Automatic Negative Thoughts (ANTs).

Learning to Manage Stress

As you climb the corporate ladder, you must learn to manage your stress. This requires both an intellectual understanding of the nature of stress (the preceding paragraphs in this chapter) and the skill to know how to channel your stress responses from the *bad* to the *good* versions of stress. This requires both a tactical approach as well as a long-term or strategic approach.

Managing Stress – Tactical

Work situations will sometimes go wrong. Often, even if the situation hasn't gone wrong, you may dream up negative *"what if…"* scenarios. These are inevitable in a career. You cannot prevent this eventuality but how you react when these happen is the key to managing stress. Here are some tips on how to handle these situations:

1. Do not act immediately, wait, think, and then act. Press the internal pause button. Take a few seconds or minutes to think before you act. This will improve the quality of action.
2. Observe your mind. What is the dominant emotion at the moment—*anger, fear, jealousy?* Be sensitive to the rise of emotions within you. Realize that actions taken under the influence of emotion are sub-optimal. As you become sensitive, you gain greater control of your emotions.
3. Watch your body. Is your breathing faster? Are the muscles of the neck, shoulders, and hands tense? Are you sweating?

4. If you feel the emotions rising, *pause. Take a few deep breaths. Walk away from the place of the event. Check your breathing and heartbeat. Wait for them to stabilize.*
5. If the cause of the stress is a mail, a wrong word said by somebody, or a gesture, *do not react.* Wait and calm yourself as pointed out in number 4 above. Nothing is gained by an instant response. If it is a nasty mail, wait for a day before you respond. If it is a wrong comment or gesture, react with SILENCE.
6. In case the stress is due to an imaginary "*what if*" situation, pause, take a deep breath, and force your mind to stop its fanciful and completely hypothetical projections. Another way is to respond *rationally* to the *"what if"* situation by coming out with Plan B and Plan C. You take the sting out of the emotion by substituting it with reason.

These tactical steps will bring down your stress levels instantly. Your subsequent actions will be from your rational rather than emotional mind. The quality of the action and the consequent reaction from the opposite party would both be better.

Managing Stress – Long-term and Strategic

The tactical steps described earlier are like first-aid, they are only a temporary fix. You need to work on yourself continually for a permanent fix to address your stress problem. It doesn't automatically happen with age—the angry young man only grows to become an angry old man. Nothing else changes.

The following steps will help you change from within:

1. Understand that the work environment you experience around you is *your creation*. It is your mind that translates the work environment into a happy or a sad one. Therefore, if you want a happy, stress-free work life, you have to work on *your mind*.
2. Practice calmness. The mind can be trained, just like the body. Spend at least 30 minutes a day sitting still and observing your normal breathing. Let thoughts come and go but continue to observe your breath. The mind will automatically calm down. Slowly these moments of calmness will percolate into your daily work life.
3. Develop a longer-term perspective. Do not expect results, immediately—give time. Have the belief that, in time, things will even out as they always do. Things that go wrong, will eventually get right.
4. Develop empathy; everything is not about you. Train your mind to think of the other party, think of how they may feel, and why they would react the way they do. Understand, accept, forgive, forget, and move on.
5. Rebuild yourself internally. Work on understanding and modifying your deepest beliefs, to suit the present circumstances. Be self-sufficient and do not always look for external endorsement. Believe that you are fine as you are.

Mastering stress is key to the *Art of the Climb*. It makes you healthier physically, calmer mentally, and more effective in dealing with situations and people. As you gain mastery over self and stress, you are readying for the ascent to the summit.

10

EVEREST BASE CAMP

$\mathcal{N}$ot all Everest climbers make it to the top. Most come up to the base camp but cannot go ahead because they are not yet ready. Allowing climbers who are not ready to attempt the final summit is dangerous not only for them but also to the others on the summit team. The same is true of corporate career climbers.

The corporate pyramid has a sharp apex. There is very little room at the top. At the very top, there is just one who bears the responsibility of the firm for the next decade or so. This person is paid a very large sum, exactly for this reason. Actions taken or not taken have an impact far beyond the tenure of the incumbent. A wrong candidate can leave a scarred organization that takes many years to recover from the damages caused.

Why is the CEO so impactful? Decisions of the top man make or scar an organization. Any serious climber in the corporate race must know this and prepare himself or herself for the challenges. Let us understand some of the key ingredients needed for the "top job."

Vision

There is an old management story that is worth repeating. I read it first decades ago, in the writings of the eminent management guru, Peter Drucker:

Walking down a village road, a man sees three stone cutters working hard at their job.

"What are you doing?" he asked the first stonecutter.

"Can't you see," the stonecutter answered, with some irritation, "I am cutting stones to earn a livelihood?"

A little ahead, he sees the second stonecutter and asks the same question. The stonecutter doesn't answer and continues with his work diligently.

The man again asks, "What are you doing?"

This time the fellow looks up and says proudly, "I am doing the best job of stonecutting in the world."

The man moves on and sees the third stonecutter and asks him the very same question.

"What are you doing, my man?"

The stonecutter looks at the man, then the stones before him, finally up to the sky and answers, "I am building a cathedral."

This is the nature of *vision*. The first stonecutter sees his work as a means of livelihood. An act that needs to be performed to keep body and soul together- *nothing more*. This is fine. He does not see beyond the immediate—the purpose or context of his work is not important to him. Many career aspirants fall into this category and there is nothing wrong.

The next stonecutter aspires for more. He seeks pride in his work. He wants to excel in it. He is an expert who defines himself within the framework of the expertise. He strives for excellence in his trade. He and others like him are the pillars on which organizations are built.

But, this is not enough to build greatness. Organizations need stronger foundations. When the third stonecutter looks up and sees the cathedral, his work becomes ethereal, almost spiritual. There is beauty, there is transcendence, and the focus is much beyond the immediate. In the mind's eye, he sees the cathedral to be built, its grandeur, its beauty. This is *vision* and it is contagious. It percolates beyond the stones he is cutting; it influences the first and second stonecutters as well. When finally the cathedral gets built, all three stonecutters look up with pride at what they accomplished together.

The true role of the CEO is to envision a great future for the organization he or she leads. Of course, the role is not limited to envisioning. The CEO must infuse this vision for the organization , into the entrails of the organization. This creates great institutions.

CEOs are hired for this rare ability of envisioning and leading the organization to greatness. This is what pays them the top dollar and what makes people talk of them in the decades to come.

But every vision does not build a cathedral. There was a disastrous attempt to build a *Third Reich*. We all know of Trump and his vision of "*make America great again.*" Ms Elizabeth Holmes, the charming start-up wonder, also had a vision for her start-up, Theranos[28] but she was willing to follow the strategy of "*fake it till you make it*" (it landed her in prison). A vision can do both harm and good. Like a rogue gene, it can corrupt the very DNA of an organization. Having a vision alone is not enough.

To be a force of good, vision needs a sister—*values*, the moral compass that regulates vision. It is the combination of vision and values that creates great organizations.

Values

Once a senior Tata executive had a proposal to save on taxes by skirting the law. The matter came up before the legendary JRD Tata, who was not in favor of this.

The tax consultant, Dinesh Vyas, was called in for an opinion and defended the proposal saying, "But, Sir, it is not illegal."

JRD is reported to have said softly, "*Not illegal, yes. But is it right?* [29]"

This is the code that JRD lived by—integrity that transcended beyond words to the spirit of the law. JRD was also renowned for his concern for society, his empathy, and his humility. These were the personal values that JRD lived by—the same values that define the actions of the companies under the Tata fold to this day.

---

[28] *Bad Blood*, John Carreyrou:https://www.panmacmillan.com/authors/john-carreyrou/bad-blood/9781509868087
[29] *The Business Ethics of J.R.D. Tata* , R.M.Lala; fdi.aurosociety.org

Three decades after his time, even the common man talks of Tata companies with reverence: If it is a Tata company, I can be sure that I will be treated fairly. While *vision* gives the destination, *values* give direction and purpose. Together, they create the organizations that last.

As you aspire to rise to the very top, it is time for you to look deep inwards and define both the vision and values you hold dear. If there is a mismatch between these and the organization you wish to lead, your ascent to the top will be uncomfortable and unsuccessful.

Exercise 10.1: Identifying Your Core Values

It is a good practice to have clarity on your deepest beliefs or core values. Look at the list of words below (Table 10.1). Each word conveys the essence of a value. The word list is not exhaustive. The last two rows are left blank for you to add words that you may like to include to the list.

Table 10.1: Core Values – Idea Words

Ambition	Fairness	Loyalty	Spirituality
Caring	Flexibility	Learning	Wealth
Collaboration	Family	Perfection	Happiness
Creativity	Freedom	Relationships	Power
Empathy	Honesty	Stability	Recognition
Excellence	Integrity	Security	Health
Leadership	Wisdom	Influencing	Risk-taking
Kindness	Competitiveness	Innovative	Peaceful

1. Look at the words above. Think of each deeply. Explore the idea behind the word. Think of or story or experience that illustrates the essence of the word.
2. Choose 10 words that are the most important for your life and career. This is difficult as all the words are "good" and you will be tempted to choose all. Resist this temptation. Ask yourself the question, *What are the words (values), I will not give up or compromise on?*
3. Personify these words or values. Think of people, companies, or institutions you deeply admire. Which of these value words would apply to them? Is that the reason you admire them?
4. Look back at your life. What were your happiest moments when you felt a sense of completeness and achievement? Was this moment a result of your practicing/experiencing any of the words/values above? For example, you may remember the happiest moment at college when you topped the class or aced a test. It is the word "*achievement*" that describes the moment.
5. Can you group the words you have chosen into a theme? For example, *empathy, influencing, and relationship* could all be part of a group called "people-oriented."
6. In this way, identify the top 3 values and themes that are most important for you in your life.

This exercise is relevant for all stages of your career. But, they are particularly important when you are looking for a top leadership role. If *integrity* is a core value for you, imagine your distress if you join a family-run organization as a CEO and are expected to do *whatever it takes,* to get a government order. Or if you believe in *empathy* and *compassion* and are expected to follow the infamous Bell Curve principle of the erstwhile GE boss, Jack Welch, of sacking the bottom 5% of your team members every year. You will either be miserable or ineffective.

Perspective

As you prepare for the CEO's job, you must develop perspective. Your actions or non-actions will impact the organization for the next decade or more. Some of your actions will be misunderstood, and some may have an adverse short-term impact but your foresight and courage will be remembered for decades after your time.

Perspective is the ability to see further than others. A first-line executive looks for the immediate impact of actions. For example, his junior has not met his target for the day and so, he calls him and shouts. "I want this done now, or else!"

His manager has a slightly larger perspective and asks the question, "Why was the result not achieved? Was skill lacking, or were resources not given?"

The GM has an even greater perspective, "Is there a larger problem here? Are we neglecting training in our company? Is there a need to revamp the supervisory training program to improve ground-level leadership?

The CEO looks even beyond: "do we have a culture problem? Have we over the years become lackadaisical? How do we instil a "must-do" culture in the company?"

Do you have a dream for the organization you would lead? Are you able to see beyond the present? Have you ever thought, "If I were the CEO, these are the changes I would bring about?" This is the first step when preparing for the top job.

Balance

A CEO's job is about trade-offs. Right trade-offs need balance: the short term with the long term, hard decisions with empathy, expediency with doing what is right, aggression with assertion, firmness with kindness, and so on. Such trade-offs are not easy to make. Balance doesn't come naturally; it must be cultivated

The top job requires this important trait—*the ability to balance.* Actions taken or not taken by the top man have repercussions even beyond the tenure of the CEO. When Elon Musk decided to sack 70% of Twitter staff, he had the power to do so, but was it wise? Did it balance the need for cost reduction with the equally important need to maintain morale? When a CEO decides to cut down the R&D budget by half (because of a bad quarter), is he balancing the needs of the future for the need of the present?

As you prepare for the ascent, steadily cultivate the personal quality of balance. Some steps to do this are:

1. Learn to understand the first-order, second-order, and third-order effects of actions. Actions have reactions beyond the obvious. The first reaction to an action is the first-order reaction. An unexpected reaction is the second order reaction, and so forth. Develop an ability to see the larger picture and the interconnected nature of things.

2. Learn to override what appears to be the obvious solution and look for what could be beyond the obvious. Have the maturity to seek the opinion of others.
3. Have the humility to accept that you are also fallible. You could be wrong.
4. Learn to handle ambiguity.

Ethics

The CEO's job comes with enormous powers. You can do good or you can scar the organization and leave it beyond repair. The lure of personal profits and fame is sometimes too enticing for CEOs. They would stoop to any extent to maximise these. Jack Welch was a legendary leader of GE. His book *Straight from the Gut* was the bible for aspiring CEOs in the nineties. Now, two decades later, we see the damage Jack Welch did to a great organization like GE. It was overstretched, its employee morale was in tatters, and a company that was the bluest of the blues fell to ignominy.[30]

There are many such examples: Carlos Ghosn, the iconic boss of Nissan and Renault had to flee Japan for the misconduct of money laundering. The complicity of the CEO and auditors of Enron in fraud is still fresh in our memory. Closer to home, we have innumerable stories of corporate fraud and misdemeanours carried out by CEOs.

A good CEO must have a strong foundation of ethics. He/she is a custodian of shareholder wealth. He is also a corporate citizen

---
[30] 27 *Power Failure – the Rise and Fall of General Electric*, William D. Cohan, 2022

with larger responsibilities to society. He also has power over people. *Ethics* provide the guardrails for the CEO to act within. He/she must not forget that the CEO's chair is a temporary one and to preserve its integrity as he/she leaves the chair is as important as delivering results while sitting on it.

If you have come this far in your career journey, it means that you have the necessary technical and managerial skills for the top job. In addition to these skills, you have sharpened your vision and values. You have also systematically worked on developing perspective, balance, and ethics. You are ready for the final ascent *but will you make it?*

11

RACE TO THE TOP

*Y*ou are almost there! You are a contender for the top job, congratulations! Here is wishing you the very best. But, there is good news and bad news:

If you are an internal candidate aiming for the CEO job, the good news is that there is an 80+ percentage chance that you would be chosen over an external candidate (*in 2018, a PwC study of CEO turnover at 2,500 of the world's largest companies found, 83% of successions involved internal candidates*[31]). Therefore, if you are ready for the job (and your company also thinks so), you are likely to get the job. There are reasons why this is so:

- You are a known commodity. Your strengths and weaknesses are known and factored in while deciding on your elevation. For example, you may be a great thinker and strategist but a bit weak in execution. The company board may consciously decide to give you the job but strengthen your hand by promoting another senior person as your deputy who is excellent in operations.

---
[31] *How Internal CEOs Succeed*; HBR Magazine, March-April, 2020

- As an internal person, you can hit the road running. Unlike an external candidate, you know the company, its bureaucracy, its strengths, and its peculiar ways. As CEO, you can negotiate these hazards far better. External candidates will take time to find their feet.
- Recruiting an internal candidate is cheaper for the company. The overall package would be lower as it would be indexed to current earnings. Furthermore, the cost of recruiting an external CEO is high (30% to 50% of the gross CTC, at the least).
- An internal candidate can get into the job much quicker, there is no notice period to wait for. The exit of the incumbent and the induction of the new CEO can be perfectly timed in the case of an internal candidate.

For all of these reasons, there is a good chance that you could get selected, *if you are a top contender.*

The bad news is that you may not be the only contender. There may be two or three other internal candidates who are equally competent and eligible. If there are two others, then your chance of making it reduces to 24% (the math – 30% chance of winning internally multiplied by 80% chance of winning against the external candidate).

Even more bad news is that you may lose out for altogether different reasons. Here is a sad story:

There were four candidates in a company identified very early on as future CEOs. They were all competent and fiercely competitive. They worked hard, inching their way up the organization. One of the contenders fell to a common hazard in companies—he got entangled in a *me-too* case. Then, there were three. They started the final lap of the CEO race.

Unfortunately, there was a major snafu—a government project failed. Someone had to be the scapegoat and the axe fell on one of the remaining three. There were only two left.

The two worked and fought for the company and with each other. Each was hopeful of making the final cut. There was even an office pool on who would win the match. The final moment of decision came. Everyone was waiting for the announcement from the Chairman.

The decision came. The Chairman was pleased to announce that his daughter, who had graduated from Harvard and had worked in McKinsey for three years, would take over as the CEO. *Often blood is a lot thicker than company loyalty and tenure.*

Sometimes, the current CEO doesn't want to let go of the power and prestige that goes with the chair. They are too addictive to be given up so easily. They use various tactics to stay on. Here is a case in point.

There was a case where the incumbent CEO planned to retire because of a failing heart condition. He instituted a nationwide CEO search and found the perfect replacement. In the meantime, his health deteriorated further and he was rushed to the US for a by-pass surgery.

After 8 weeks, he was back with a renewed heart, feeling fully rejuvenated. He felt fit and wanted his toy back. He cancelled the CEO search and decided to stay on.

Sometimes, the current CEO uses more subtle ways to hang on to the chair. He/she convinces the board that there is no one ready for the job as yet. This is done in various ways: downplaying the work of a possible successor, forcing a potential successor to retire prematurely or getting two potential successors to fight with each other and declaring that to retain both in the company, the present CEO should stay on for a few more years.

There are also strategies for creating bogies: an aggressive competitor, possible government change that requires internal stability, an IPO, or an incomplete project. The CEO chair is so seductive that once having got a taste of it, letting go becomes difficult. The incumbent tries his/her best to stay on. Is it any wonder that an old 80-year-old man with a stutter and fading memory wants to cling on as the CEO of the most powerful country in the world, for another four years? This is a political example and there are many in the corporate world as well.

Assuming you have cleared all these hurdles and have the top job, congratulations! But be aware that the going is not going to be easy at all. There are the special snakes that lurk in the CEO's office. Both internal and external CEOs face challenges although the nature of the challenges may be different. Let us look at these:

The internally promoted CEO

CEOs who have advanced from within, face several challenges as per a recent HBR article[32] on the subject.

- **Operating in the shadows of your past**: People in the company (your peers, subordinates, and bosses) know

---

[32] *How Internal CEOs Succeed*; HBR, March-April, 2020

you and have pre-formed notions about how you would behave in situations. Your track record is known as also your operating style. In your new role, as you take on new responsibilities, your behavior will change. What was important in an earlier role may be less important given your new job and altered perspectives. Your colleagues will be surprised by and may resent the *new you*. It is for you to explain to them that your new job demands change. Many also may feel that you are unprepared and would be waiting to see you fail. They are just waiting to say, "See, I told you so." To counter such assumptions, you must consciously act and demonstrate that you are now different from your previous roles. You will have to try harder to legitimize your promotion.

- **Making tough calls that may disappoint supporters**: You are now CEO of the whole company which requires you to go beyond earlier affiliations. *I am from marketing, I am a finance guy, or I am from this SBU*—such identities are no longer valid or appropriate. You may need to take difficult decisions such as closing down a business, creating structural changes, reprioritizing investment, or changing policies. These may disappoint erstwhile supporters but for the good of the company, they may be needed.
- **Supervising former peers (maybe even bosses)**: Most internal CEOs will have to lead people who were former peers or even bosses. This can be tricky and must be handled with maturity and care. You will have to work with and supervise erstwhile competitors who lost out on the top job and you may have clashed with some in the past. You have to confront these with maturity, empathy, and firmness.

The external CEO

CEOs who come from other companies have a different set of problems. They would have to work with others who have lost out on the race. The new CEO brings in a different set of cultural values that the organization may not be prepared for. Here is an example:

A senior executive director, a long-term Maruti employee was brought in as CEO of a mid-sized manufacturing organization. He realized quickly that the new organization was everything Maruti was not in terms of systems, quality orientation, people management, and shopfloor practices. In fact, the company board had head-hunted him precisely for this reason; they wanted to change their organization for the better. The task ahead was very difficult because culture and style are the most difficult to change.

This new CEO's principal task was to change the company culture over time through a systematic and well-orchestrated change management program.

Creating Change – the principal task

The CEO is principally the change agent. It is easy to give up and continue with the old culture. But you have been hired to bring about change and you must resolve to do this. It involves working with the board, creating allies of your senior team members, creating internal change agents, and diligently working on your change agenda. This is your job as the CEO. Here are some steps to succeed:

1. Have a firm resolve and a clear direction of where you want to go. Share your vision for the company and its people with all. Let them know and own this vision. Encourage innovation. Allow people the freedom to think and express their ideas for growing the business.
2. Take bold steps and don't wait too long to show that you mean business. Don't let the organization become a prisoner of its past. If businesses need to be closed, *close them*. If a new path is to be taken, *take it*.
3. Quickly put together a team of performers. Don't hesitate to take tough decisions regarding people, structures, and positions.
4. Keep your eye on the cash. Make sure you have plenty of it. Find out where your cash is locked up and direct efforts to release this. It is the best defence against bad markets, difficult customers, and adamant suppliers. Nothing aborts a change management project, more than cash flow problems.
5. Feel the pulse of your employees. Win them to your side. Energize them with your enthusiasm and hope.
6. *Communicate, communicate, communicate* ! Let people know what you are doing and why. Let the communication be two-way. Create a channel where anyone in the company can reach out to you. Walk around the offices and factories and talk to people. Hear and feel the pulse of the people.
7. Meet customers, employees, suppliers and partners and get to hear their voices first-hand. Do not create layers that muffle these voices from you.

8. Establish your equation with the board. Let them be on your side. Do not hesitate to tell them the truth about the organization as you perceive it. Tough decisions will need the board's overt and covert approval. Here is an illustrative story:

A new CEO joined a company with the mandate to turn around the company. In the first few weeks, he realised that the company had a very poor work culture, a recalcitrant union, and burgeoning employee costs. The only way to set things right was to attack the employee/work culture problem head-on. This would have serious short term consequences.

The CEO approached the board with a plan. He asked for a free hand to deal with the labour and the union. He asked for a sixty day time window, with a possibility of strikes/lock down and profit loss. He asked the board to consider the loss as an investment for the future. The board agreed to the plan, albeit reluctantly.

The CEO alerted customers, senior managers and even the labor department. He took a tough stand against the unions/labor. The company went through a lock down for a period of 45 days. When the company opened at the end of this dark period, it had a new labor agreement signed and better work culture. In the next five years, the company emerged stronger, grew in both the top and bottom lines.

It was a bold strategy that required courage and resolve. That is what the CEO was hired for. He delivered!

9. Look for potential time bombs in the company. These could be wrong accounting practices, unclean balance

sheets, pending or potential litigation, failing factory infrastructure, or impending government legislation that could be disastrous for your business.
10. Above all give yourself and the organization time to absorb and implement the change. In the enthusiasm to succeed, do not burn yourself and the team out.

Learning new skills

Till now, the rising professional has been delivering results and driving the bottom line. As MD & CEO, there are new challenges. The CEO becomes the face of the company. The buck stops at the CEO's desk. All acts of omission and commission of the company are the responsibility of the CEO. He/she has to ensure good corporate governance.

The Cadbury Report (1992) has provided guidelines and recommendations for raising the standards of corporate governance as well as financial reporting and auditing in organizations. The CEO must be familiar with these.

The MD & CEO should understand the role of the board committees and those of the independent directors heading the audit and nomination committees. These, as well as ensuring that CSR and ESG requirements are meticulously met, are the responsibilities of the CEO.

For the new CEO, these may be unfamiliar territories but these must be learned.

It is lonely at the top

The CEO's job is not all hunky dory, *it is lonely at the top*. The CEO's chair isolates you. You are alone as you grapple with a lot of things, both short and long-term. Often, you have to keep secrets even from your closest aides. You have competitors all around you who are masquerading as friends. You have sycophants who blind you with praise. Many are waiting for you to fail.

How do you cross the minefield? How do you survive the CEO years? How long will you survive as a CEO? Will you succeed? These are questions that will plague your mind.

You must learn to manage this *isolation*. Here are a few tips:

1. Now that you are CEO, reconcile with the fact that even your closest friends in the company will behave differently with you. This comes with the territory and you have to deal with it.
2. Learn to be comfortable alone. Many need company all the time. As you come closer and closer to the CEO chair, train yourself to be your own counsel.
3. Cultivate external counsel. This could be other CEOs, persons you trust, or even professional coaches. These are persons who have no personal axe to grind and would provide you with the forum to let out your feelings and doubts.

CEO longevity and its lessons

A survey among best-performing CEOs[33] in Fortune 500 companies reveals that there is a pattern in the tenure and success of CEOs. On average, *the best-performing* CEOs spend 15 years on the job as against about 10 years for all CEOs. The last few years of tenure are often the glorious period in the case of the best-performing CEOs.

CEOs go through a *honeymoon period* which lasts about one year. In the case of US presidents, for example, for the first 90 days, the incumbent is left alone by the press and the opposition. Normally, company CEOs get a year for them to find their feet.

This is followed by, what is described as, the *sophomore slump*—a period of two to three years. During this period, the exuberance of the honeymoon is replaced by the unmet expectations of the media, markets, and employees. Many CEOs are not able to survive this phase.

The next three to five years are considered the *recovery years* when the CEO settles down and his/her actions are seen to bear fruits. Unfortunately, this is followed by many years of complacency, when things settle down to sameness.

If the CEO has survived all these and still enjoys the board's confidence, the next five years could be the *glorious period* of the tenure. He/she has established a reputation, there is nothing left to prove, and is free to do the real things that matter to leave his/her mark in the annals of the company.

---

[33] *The CEO Lifecycle*; HBR Nov-Dec 2019

All careers will end but life has to go on. You may have made it to the top or you may have maxed out somewhere along the way. In either case, you will have to, at some point, get off the career bandwagon and resume your post-career life. An important part of the *Art of the Climb* is the planning and preparation for this phase as well. Read on…

12

NEW BEGINNINGS

*S*ometimes, in a heady career, one forgets that there are another twenty or thirty years of life left after the career. You will no longer have the position of *Vice President, General Manager* or even *CEO*. You will no longer have the umbrella of an organization to give you succour. You have lost the membership to the *club* that was your organization—a club to retreat to with buddies, for a sense of belonging. You are alone to face this new post-retirement world.

Often, this is too much to bear for many career professionals. They are just not able to adjust to a world where they are no longer in the decision-making chair, when there is no one to do their bidding, and their *centre* appears to have lost its centricity. No wonder many career professionals wither away after retirement. They become pale shadows of their earlier selves—bitter, unhappy, and looking for any opportunity to relive their past glory. This is sad.

Planning for retirement is an integral part of your career journey. If you manage to climb the mountain, you must be able to climb back to tell the tale. If you have spent all your energy reaching the top and destroyed all your gear in the climb, how will you come down to earth?

Let us discuss the problem and then look for solutions.

The problem of life centring

We are individuals with no identity to begin with. As we grow in life, we create identities based on family, country, race, religion, and profession. These define us. Often, we identify so completely with these identities that we forget our core. This is why an army man still calls himself a Brigadier or Colonel even after retirement or a retired corporate honcho still refers to himself as a GM (retd.), XYZ company.

Often this identity is created at the expense of other identities that define us. For example, the Brigadier may also be a musician, golfer, or an author. But during the height of career-centredness, all other identities are subsumed under the powerful influence of the career identity.

One of the ways of countering this is to consciously create and nurture different identities while in a career. This not only makes you a more interesting person but also provides you with an alternate base to build your post-retirement life. There are many stellar examples:

Nandan Nilekani had a great innings as a founding member of the hugely successful company, Infosys. Post-retirement from that role, he moved into a larger arena. He used his knowledge of technology and his expertise in organizations to bring about instruments for social change. Working with the government, he conceived and created the Aadhaar, ONDC and India Stack projects, the backbones of Digital India.

Gurcharan Das was the CEO of an MNC. After his tenure, he transformed into a successful author.

Bill Gates after building Microsoft retired and focussed his energy on his foundation. His efforts could rid the world of killer diseases in distant parts of the globe.

These are famous examples. There are countless others of people who after a successful corporate career, went on to create meaningful lives. Often, the world remembers them not for their career but for their post-career achievements.

If I look back at my own life, I retired from a corporate career at the age of 52. I then started a consulting business, earned a PhD, read, taught, and travelled the world with my wife. I recreated my post-retirement world, completely different from the earlier corporate world I lived in for nearly three decades. If I could do this, anybody can.

Post Career Planning

The post-career life must be a happy one. Otherwise, the thirty to forty-odd years spent in it become worthless. How does one plan for a happy life after a career?

The way to do this is not after the career *but when in it*. You must always maintain a balance in your life. Do not give it all to a career. It is not worth it. A bad economy, a recession, a bad boss, a corporate takeover—any of these can take away the bottom of your world. If your whole life is only standing on this weak foundation of a career, it can be catastrophic after you exit from work.

Ideally, there must be three or four compartments into which you package your life. One compartment is your career. The next is your "other interests," *separate from your career*. These could be a hobby, a passion, or an alternative skill. Family and friends make up another important compartment that gets neglected in a busy career. Nurture these alternate themes of your life, *while in a career*. If Pandit Nehru could write, think and romance while running the country, so can you and I. These alternate themes become the pillars on which you build your post-retirement life. You must remember that your career is just one of the pillars, albeit an important one. But, *only one of the pillars*.

The most important compartment you must work on and nurture is *yourself*. See yourself as different from your identity as a career professional. You do not need a career to define who you are. Be complete in yourself. See your career as just another costume that you wear.

The primary pillars

The three primary pillars on which you build your post-career life are *health*, *wealth* and *purpose*. Without health there is no peace of mind; without sufficient wealth, you are too distracted to live a happy life; and of course, without purpose, your life is a ship without a rudder. You must work on strengthening each of these pillars while you are in your career. If neglected during the career, it is near impossible to build these after retirement. Here is an illustrative but apocryphal story:

There was an ancient country that has a strange custom. They had kings by rotation, each serving for three years only. During his reign, the king had a life of total luxury and pleasure. But after the three years of reign, the king was banished to a wicked forest that had unspeakable horrors. Everyone dreaded to be king but the lure of three years of luxury was tantalising for many.

So, one king followed another till one day, a new king was throned. He had his three years of pleasure. The last few months of the reign were remaining. This was the period of gloom for kings because they dreaded what was in store for them. But this king seemed different as he was looking forward to the wicked forest!

Everyone was intrigued about how this king was so different. Normally, the last few months were the worst and kings had to be literally dragged out and forced into the forest. But this king seemed to be looking forward to the horrors.

Not able to understand the mystery, the king's minister asked him, "Sire, aren't you afraid of what is in store for you? How can you be so cheerful?"

The king replied with a laugh, "Yes, I was afraid when I started my reign because I didn't know what awaited me. So, I sent out spies to find out what was so dreadful in the wicked forest. My spies told me that the forest was wild, with no fruits or flowers, just fearful creatures that devoured men." The king continued, "I then sent my armies to clear the forest and kill the wild creatures.

I also sent my friends and family ahead to set up a home and plant flowers and fruit trees. So now, I am going to an enchanted forest, with wildflowers, fruits, family, and friends to welcome me."

The world that you move into, after your career, can be an enchanted one if you make it one, *while you are in a career.* Let us see how to prepare:

Strengthen the primary pillars

Longevity extends *old age,* not youth. The essence of post-retirement living is keeping the qualities of youth, *energy, enthusiasm,* and *hope,* alive at every age while scrupulously avoiding the foibles of youth—drinking to get drunk, living dangerously, and behaving as if there is no tomorrow. This requires a healthy mind and body.

Preserve health

We are endowed with a wonderful, self-healing, and intelligent learning machine, our mind and body. We have a lifetime to preserve and train it to ensure it stays fit till the last day. But, the tragedy is that we take this machine for granted, and abuse it, leaving it unfit for use when we need it the most.

We forget that our body can renew and heal itself, often without doctors, tests, and medicine, *if left alone.* It just needs good food, rest, and exercise. Our careers so consume us that we deny ourselves even this simple indulgence. We punish it with 12-hour work days, no sleep and dollops of stress just to add a few zeros to the already burgeoning bottom lines of our companies. Is it a wonder that as we near retirement, our bodies have given up?

Now comes the mind. It is the fount of the emotional you. It makes you sad, angry, fearful, and jealous. Each of these emotions corrodes you till you are left a bitter shell of the real you. Your mind must make you happy—not sad and angry. A career gives ample opportunities for both emotions. Choose the happy emotion.

Finally, the intellect. It is the software that runs your body and mind. Keep it sharp. Feed it with new ideas. A mark of youth is the sharpness of intellect. But this is not the prerogative of youth. Keep your intellect razor sharp through retirement and the life thereafter.

Conserve Wealth

Wealth is not an absolute measure but a relative one. Wealth is the difference between what you earn and what you need. If your needs are more than what you earn, you are not wealthy, how much ever you earn. As you move into retirement, your earning may come down but you can still be wealthy if you moderate your needs.

Having said that, you still need to plan your wealth for the decades when you don't have active earnings. Here are some guidelines to follow:

1. Be debt free by the time of retirement. If not totally free of debt at least try to have liquid assets that would cover your debt comfortably. This gives you peace of mind.
2. Let your money work for you, even after retirement. Plan your investments in a manner where the interest/dividend

earned can cover your expenses comfortably. Taking the help of a money manager is useful.
3. Strive for financial independence. You should not have to depend on children or others for any of your needs.
4. Build an alternative earning stream. This could be a hobby that gives revenue, a business, royalty payment streams, or any other. It is good to have money flowing in, however small, even after retirement.
5. Progressively reduce your needs. Avoid vanity spending—the flashy car that you will not take out, designer clothes or accessories that you won't have occasions to show off, or even that latest model of the iPhone which is just another phone.

Derive Purpose

Make your retirement years the most purposeful phase of your career. You have the maturity and wisdom of age, you have the knowledge and skills from a career and you also have the time. Don't fritter away this treasure by retreating from life and the world. Don't spend the time reminiscing the past or cursing the present or even worrying about the uncertain future. It is your time to leave a mark in the world.

You have had a lifetime of learning and earning in a career and now is payback time. Dedicate your retirement years to *a purpose* and you would have found the key to happiness.

SUMMARY OF CHAPTERS

Chapter 1: The First Steps

1. The purpose of this book is to help a person navigate the ups and downs of a corporate career and come out winning.
2. A career is a long journey and this path can be winding and treacherous. It requires technique and finesse to succeed. That is why the book is called *Art of the Climb*.
3. Goals are important in planning a career. You must know what you seek from a career. These would be different for different people. You must set your career goals, frequently re-examine them, and correct the course of your career as needed.
The Career Goals Assessment, Exercise 1.1, is a useful tool for evaluating your career progression.
4. Your career path must be aligned with the goal you have set. Exercise 1.2 helps you check this alignment. Your career goals must be aspirational but at the same time realistic.
5. A career is made up of a series of jobs and/or roles either in one company or in multiple companies. Changing jobs or job roles should be a strategic choice.

Chapter 2: Is There a Job For You?

1. This chapter is about the process of searching for a job. The irony is that while there are people in search of jobs, there are employers in search of candidates. Both don't seem to find each other easily.
2. The reason for this is that both the job seeker and the employer approach the issue from different angles. As a job seeker, you must understand this difference and work around it.
3. The interview is the process of discovery, both for the candidate and the employers. There must be a cultural fit between the company and the candidate. As a job seeker, you must use the interview process to understand this cultural fit.
4. Salary negotiations are an integral part of the interview. This must be handled carefully. Your attempt must be to get fitted in the upper end of the salary band for the position.
5. Designations and span of control are also important in a job. The interview is the place to clarify and fix these issues.
6. Reference checking is the final stage before the hiring decision. Ensure that you have persons who would give you a good reference. Such referees should be cultivated. Exercise 2.1 helps you create good referees for your job search.

Chapter 3: When Do You Leave a Job?

1. This chapter deals with the subject of job change in the pursuit of a career. It discusses the need for a job change, the reasons why you would want to change the job and the timing of it.
2. A framework called the Earning & Learning (E&L) framework is introduced to help the professional decide if and when to leave a job. Every job should provide *learning* opportunities as well as *earning* opportunities. It is time to consider a change if either is missing.
3. You can use the checklist Table 3.1 to evaluate your learning and earning. These are measures or markers to track your learning and earning from your present job.
4. The concept of a *career pivot* is introduced. This is when you make a sharp change in your career trajectory. Career pivots challenge and prepare you for higher level jobs in the future. Several case studies are provided, to explain the concept.

Chapter 4: Rungs of the Ladder

1. Organizational grade structures and designations can be confusing. As they are not standardized, one never knows the equivalence of these across companies. This can result in career blunders.
2. How do you know whether you are getting a higher level or not when you join another company? This chapter clarifies this dilemma.
3. This chapter explains the rungs of the corporate ladder. It clarifies that there are five real management levels in an organization: board, top management, senior management, middle management, and junior management.
4. The responsibilities of each of these levels are explained:
   a. The *board* is the representative of the share/stakeholders. Independent board members are responsible for protecting the interests of the minority shareholders.
   b. The *top management* is responsible for preserving the values of the company, providing perspective, and ensuring the present and future earnings of the company. They are responsible for the several businesses that make up the company.
   c. The *senior management* is the layer responsible for the P&L of the SBUs, providing leadership for functions and is the penultimate layer to the top.
   d. *Middle management* is the strategic thinking and executing layer. They are responsible for translating the long-term vision into businesses that deliver results.

e. *Junior management* is the operating layer of the company.
5. This chapter provides a helicopter view of organizations and their management structures.

Chapter 5: Does Your Boss Like You

1. This chapter is about managing bosses. Bosses are an inevitable part of your career. How you manage them makes a big difference both to your career as well as your peace of mind.
2. For most employees, the immediate boss *is* the company. How the employee experiences the boss, determines the employee's feelings towards the company. It does not matter how good the company is - if the immediate boss is unfriendly and unfair to the employee, then the company is perceived as unfair and unfriendly.
3. Bosses are the same—good, bad, or indifferent. This chapter gives vignettes of different types of bosses you may encounter in your career.
4. How your boss treats you depends on how you behave and interact. Instead of lamenting on a bad boss, introspect on what you need to do to get your boss to like you.
5. The chapter provides guidelines on making yourself acceptable to your boss.

Chapter 6: The Indian Rope Trick

1. Many things may go wrong in a career. You will face headwinds. There would be unfortunate events that could derail your career. These are referred to as *snakes* in this book and this chapter is about managing such eventualities.
2. This chapter also explains how you can convert a career hazard into an opportunity—*a ladder*—and come out as a winner.
3. A hazard could be a wrong start, an industry collapse, a failed project, or any other. How you manage these makes a big difference both to your career success as well as your peace of mind.
4. The chapter discusses the eventuality of job loss. This can happen in any career. The methods of preparing for job loss and the actions needed to overcome this are also discussed.
5. The importance of networking is explained in this chapter. Some steps to build powerful networks are also enumerated.

Chapter 7: Results Matter

1. Success comes to those who deliver results, *consistently*. This is the message of this chapter. Unless you deliver on your KPIs, you cannot grow in a career, however brilliant or knowledgeable you may be.
2. The results are, (1) profits and growth at the business head level and (2) functional goals at departmental levels. Irrespective of your functional area or department, your growth in the company depends on your achieving these results.
3. The chapter discusses the way to consistently achieve results. It suggests a framework consisting of three cornerstones: *competence, method* and *positivity*. Competence is your *skill and knowledge* to do the job. A method is the *way* you do the job and positivity is your *attitude* to work and life that enables you to excel in your job.
4. This chapter introduces a technique, O-KR (Objectives-Key Results), for achieving results. This technique is used by leading companies like Intel, Google, and Facebook.
5. This chapter also suggests that it is not only enough to achieve results, but you must also enable others to achieve their results. This includes peers, subordinates, and bosses. If you enable all to achieve results you will be seen as a very valuable person ready for top leadership.

Chapter 8: Behaviour Matters, Even More

1. This chapter shows that negative workplace habits are responsible for the downfall of many professionals. Brilliant careers are often halted or seriously impaired by bad behavior. However smart or effective you are, if you behave poorly with colleagues, your career would be affected.
2. This chapter describes different types of bad behaviors and their effect on careers. These are *uncontrolled anger*, *negativity*, *being pessimistic*, etc. These are explained through stereotypes or vignettes that bring such patterns to life.
3. The chapter also helps you recognize such disruptive patterns in others and yourself.
4. The chapter lists positive behaviors that help careers. Some of these are: *smiling, listening, being proactive,* and *praising*. The most important positive behavior is being ethical and this chapter talks about the importance of ethics in careers.

Chapter 9: Stress-The Career Killer

1. This chapter discusses the issue of stress which is the cause of many career downfalls.
2. This chapter explains the nature of stress. It is a primordial response of the mind and body to danger—real or imaginary. Stress response differs from person to person.
3. Stress is caused by an internal response to an external event. To deal with the stress, one has to look inwards. One has to deal with stressful events with maturity and calm.
4. There are two types of stress—good stress and bad stress. The former is like the power in a coiled spring; great results are produced if the power is used well. Bad stress is like an overstretched rubber band; it can snap.
5. The chapter gives guidelines on dealing with workplace stress. There are short-term tactics to tackle stress. These are watching your mind and emotions, pausing before taking action, etc. There are also long-term measures to tackle stress which require you to work on yourself internally to alter your personality.

Chapter 10: Everest Base Camp

1. This chapter reminds us that not all climbers make it to the top. Most come up to the base camp but cannot go ahead because they are not yet ready.
2. CEOs are paid so highly because their actions impact their organizations for decades after their time. Therefore, to qualify for the top job, a professional has to be prepared.
3. Organizations need a vision to prosper and grow. The job of the CEO is to co-create and inspire employees with this vision. While being aspirational, the vision should be realistic. This requires a delicate balance.
4. In addition to vision, to qualify as a CEO, you must have guiding values. These values form the guardrail that ensures that the organization stays on its chosen path to growth.
5. To succeed as a CEO, the incumbent must develop two other qualities, perspective, balance and ethics.

Chapter 11: Race to the Top

1. This chapter is addressed to the professional who is close to reaching the top.
2. The chapter reminds us that If you are an internal candidate seeking an elevation as a CEO, there is an 80+ percentage chance that you would be chosen over an external candidate.
3. The challenges of an internal CEO are different from that of an external CEO. While the internal CEO can hit the road running, the external CEO may take some time to find his/her feet. The internal CEO has to fight perceptions as they are judged by the shadows of their past. They may have to supervise those who were peers or even seniors. This is a challenge.
4. The job of the CEO is a lonely one. One of the challenges is to be comfortable with this aloneness. Further, the CEO has to learn to be wary of sycophants. Choosing the right counsel and avoiding such sycophants is essential to succeed as a CEO.
5. A survey among best-performing CEOs in Fortune 500 companies reveals that there is a pattern in the tenure and success of CEOs. On average *the best-performing* CEOs spend 15 years in the job as against about 10 years for all CEOs.

Chapter 12: New Beginnings

1. This chapter discusses life after a career and preparing for it while in a career. There are another twenty or thirty years or more of life left after the career. You will no longer have the position of *Vice President*, *General Manager*, or even *CEO*. You have to learn to manage this phase of life.
2. We are individuals with no identity to begin with. As we grow in life we create identities based on family, country, race, religion, and profession. These define us. Often, we identify so completely with these identities that we forget our core.
3. The post-career life must be a happy one. Otherwise, the thirty-odd years spent in it become worthless. This chapter helps plan for a happy life after a career. Longevity extends old age, *not youth*. This is the tragedy. The essence of post-retirement living is extending youthfulness through old age. Keeping the qualities of youth, *energy, enthusiasm,* and *hope,* alive at every age is key to a happy post-career life. Finally, the chapter tells us that you have had a lifetime of learning and earning in a career, and now is payback time. Dedicate your retirement years to *a purpose* and you would have found the key to happiness.

ABOUT THE AUTHOR

Dr. C. Venugopal, MD & CEO of Krysalis Consultancy Services Private Limited (www.krysalisco.com), an author, consultant and coach has worked with hundreds of professionals helping them grow and develop into successful achievers in their chosen fields. As an IIT engineer, with post graduate qualifications in management and a PhD in management, he has decades of experience in corporate India in senior positions.

He writes and lectures on management topics and coaches professionals to become better versions of themselves. He is the author of two best selling books, *BYOB—Be Your Own Boss*, a book on entrepreneurship and *Unchained*, a book on how to break your shackles and achieve your full potential.

Venugopal lives in Chennai and can be contacted at cvenugopal@gmail.com. You can also visit his website, www.cvenugopal.com.

www.ingramcontent.com/pod-product-compliance
Lightning Source LLC
LaVergne TN
LVHW041949070526
838199LV00051BA/2952